GW00597261

Best Wrshr

Paddy Faley

The Life and Rhymes of Paddy Faley

The Life and Rhymes of Paddy Faley

Author
Paddy Faley

Published by
As Dúchas Dóchas

The Life and Rhymes of Paddy Faley

Published in Ireland in 2003 by

As Dúchas Dóchas,
Old County Council Offices,
Bishop Street,
Co. Limerick,
Ireland.

Tel: +353 (0)69 62215
Fax : +353 (0)69 62269

Web: http://www.asduchasdochas.pro.ie
E-mail: asduchasdochas@eircom.net

Author
Paddy Faley

ISBN: 0-9541802-4-0

Front Cover Photo: Bridie Murphy
Title Page Photo: Bridie Murphy

CONTENTS

FOREWORD

It is an honour and immense privilege to be asked to pen a foreword for this wonderful and most welcome book, aptly titled "The Life and Rhymes of Paddy Faley".

Paddy is an unique person. Though in his mid eighties he is very much in touch with national and international affairs. He possesses a rare talent for composing, in a matter of minutes, a ballad or poem about a character, team, place or happening.

He is a very hospitable and caring person and visitors to his homestead are assured of a "Céad Míle Failte" as the kettle is permanently on the boil. He didn't earn the title "The Mayor of Glenbawn" for nothing.

In this book he has expressed pride, love and passion for his native place which he has chronicled for posterity and offers a revealing insight into a way of life that is fast disappearing even from rural Ireland. The people are living through a period of transformation that has no precedent in our chequered history.

Paddy did not have an easy passage in this rocky road of life. Born in 1919, he married at the age of 33 but became a widower 10 years later. But Paddy was resilient; he knuckled down and reared his family of five daughters of whom he can feel justly proud.

It is my earnest hope that this flagship book will be read and heeded by many of our youth and thereby sow the seed of a lasting legacy for generations to enjoy and perhaps emulate.

Seán Murphy
Winner of 5 McNamee Awards

Acknowledgements are due to the following publications where some of these articles first appeared:

Ballyguiltenane Rural Journals

Athea Parish Journal

Loughill/Ballyhahill Parish Newsletter

All Write by An Post

Desmond News

Verses from Owvaun

Recollections of our Native Valley

Some poems have been broadcast on Live at 3 on RTE, RLO, Galtee Kerry Radio, Clare FM, Cork Country Sound and West Limerick Community Radio.

DEDICATION:

To my five daughters – Peg, Helen, Bridie, Gerardine and Philomena for their care. A special word of thanks to Peg who put a lot of work into compiling this book.
To my thirteen grandchildren who give me joy in my old age.

Copyright 2003

Grateful thanks to
Estuary Credit Union
Limerick Co. Council
for some sponsorship towards costs

A WORD ABOUT THE AUTHOR

Paddy Faley was born in 1919 in Glasha, Athea, Co. Limerick, one of a family of six. He moved three miles east to Glenbawn, Ballyhahill on his 40th birthday and has lived there since. He wrote his first poem that night called "The Home I left Behind." Since then he has written lots of poems and plays as well as lots of articles on life growing up in the 30's, 40's and 50's in West Limerick. Growing up under the shadow of emigration, though he never experienced emigration himself, inspired him to write lots of poems on the pain of being forced to leave one's homeland.

He went to school at the age of seven to Ballyguiltenane for five years finishing with two more years in Knocknagorna before he left at fourteen years of age to go working in the bog. Later on he was employed by Limerick County Council where he worked as a Road Ganger until he retired at sixty six years of age.

He married Ellen White, Templeglantine in 1952 and had five daughters but was widowed after ten years.

He is a great fan of the Radio, especially local radio, where he is often asked to contribute some of his poems and yarns and is best known for "Minding the House."

He joined in Joe Harrington's Rambling Tour of Britain on three occasions in recent years. He contributes to all local journals annually and was a founding member of the Ballyguiltenane Rural Journal, edited by T.J. O' Donoghue where many of the items in this book first appeared.

He won several prizes in "Dear Sir or Madam" – a programme on Radio Éireann in the 1960's. He has won many medals and trophies for recitations and newly composed ballads in Fleadh Ceoil competitions and Féiles in West Limerick over the past years.

The Lord has been generous and my position has improved
And from my home there in the mountain reluctantly I have moved
With my loving wife and children I've settled in Glenbawn
With a slated roof above me and a tidy little farm.
The church and school convenient and the road right to the door
Running water in the tap – how could I ask for more?
But still my thoughts go wandering back and to cry I am inclined
When I think of friends in Glasha and the home I left behind.

For three and ninety Christmas nights the candles burned bright
And shone through its cheerful windows the travellers to guide
No bolts or bars did hold the door 'gainst strangers kith or kin
There was a céad míle fáilte for all to come within.
But now alas 'tis sad to see the cold and dreary look
No living sound within its walls that once with laughter shook
For my parents they are dead and gone their peace with God to find
'Tis as silent as a graveyard now – the home I left behind.

I had such loving parents and each other did assist
They lived in blissful harmony and no quarrels did exist
They were hard working and industrious
and whatever tired they'd be
They never would retire at night without saying the rosary.
So now like them upon our knees to God above we pray
To follow their example and imitate their way
One special request we ask the Lord that in time to come we'll find
We've made this home as happy as the home we left behind.

Memories of Glasha

Glashapullagh or Glasha is the name of a comparatively small townland in the parish of Athea, in the west of Co. Limerick. It means
nothing to a lot of people but to me it is a place held sacred in my
memory. I grew up here with Rooskagh Hill, towering high to the
south-east along by South Keale and Cratloe. West of Athea stands the
hill of Knockathea and further west is Knockanure. The ruins of the
old church could be seen from our doorstep. To the west we could see
Knockanore, overlooking Ballybunion, and not too far to the north
stood Knocknaleague in Glenagragra. A little to the east we viewed
Knocknaclugga where remnants of snow remained long after it had
vanished everywhere else. Directly in front of our house was the long
back of Knockadullaun with its valuable turbary. On this mountainside was a long stretch of marshland known as the "White Vein"
caused, I believe, by a powerful spring of water gushing up and
becoming trapped in the area around it. Anybody foolish enough to
attempt to walk its shaking surface would be taking his life in his
hands because if the soft skin broke it seemed bottomless underneath.
It was the haunt of wild geese, duck and snipe and well known to the
fowlers who frequented it.

Here in Glasha, in a thatched homestead in 1919, I bawled my first
cry after getting a slap in the backside from old Nurse Foley of Athea,
who delivered me. Maternity hospitals were not resorted to then, only
in complicated cases, and there were few that needed them. A lot of
babies were born without even a qualified midwife and a handy
woman in the locality would act as midwife and successfully do the
job. Indeed my own mother was one of those women herself.

I'll go back a bit in history to the time when the first of my ancestors
came to Glasha. Situated here was a green fertile portion of land,
hemmed in on all sides by the brown mountainside like an oasis in the
desert, belonging to George Lynch. This portion of land was separated from the main farm, which was bordering the Kerryline and

extending eastwards for a long way.

George invited my grandfather, who was only a short time married to Ellen Sheehan and living in some shack in Templeathea, to build a house in this part of the farm. Even though it was a remote place my grandfather gladly consented and took up residence there in 1866 when my own father was only nine days old.

Probably the reason for offering him the site of the house was twofold; he was a contractor, having many miles of roads to keep in repair as well as the construction of new ones and he knew he could expect the labourer on his land to work for his employment. Thus it was and it served my grandfather well to find himself in constant employment. Not alone did he work at Lynchs but his sons, my father and my Uncle Dan worked there too, when they became able. Thus a close bond of friendship was built up and prevailed between the Lynchs and the Faleys from the first day my grandfather came to Glasha to the present day, each family holding the other in high regard.

George's son James carried on in the contracting business after his father's death. He was a man of quiet disposition and when he died early in life his widow Bridget carried on the business until she handed over authority to her son George, who had inherited the quiet nature and great sense of humour of his father. Many is the happy night I spent at his homestead in my teens and later. His wife Nora Barrett, or "Noan" as we called her, would often visit Dalton's next door for a chat and while she was out George would join in every frolic and caper which we young lads participated in around the large kitchen, more often than not in his stocking feet. Noan, on returning, sometimes noticed George's heels appearing through the socks, the soles of which he had worn out on the flagstoned floor hopping around. She'd start giving out to George who sat as mute as could be trying to suppress a smile.

I remember one night he sported a black eye after getting a belt from Sonny Reidy while playing a game of balloons. One half of the company assembled playing against the other side to get the balloons, striking them over our heads to the other end of the kitchen. Sonny was bound to hit someone always - accidentally, according to himself, but his misdemeanours were always enjoyed and taken in good fun.

Getting back to my birthplace; many long years before my grandfather came to live here, this spot must have housed other people as there are remains of the fences enclosing an oval shaped portion of land fenced in three different divisions. The plots and ridges in which they tilled the crops were still showing. It looked as if the crops failed and the ridges were left un-dug - maybe in the famine times - and the people who cultivated them sailed out in coffin ships to America. There was a story told locally of a woman about to die in America who told of treasure being hidden in a corner of the particular place that I'm writing about.

Long before this time the place must have been inhabited because I discovered that five feet beneath the surface about one hundred yards from where our homestead stood, ran a road about ten feet wide with small flat stones. Where it started or finished I was not sure but year after year we uncovered some more of it as we cut the turf overhead.

Another interesting find, five feet from the surface, was a "sliotar" made from cow's hair, rolled in a ball between the hands and covered in the most expert way by the long "slander" of the cow's tail woven around it.

When my grandparents came to settle in their new home the nearest spring well was the "Paddock Well", a long distance away. One evening as my grandfather returned from work, during a long spell of drought, he noticed water in a cow track not far from the house. Having a spade on his shoulder he dug a hole where he saw the water and to his delight he found a spring flowing underneath. Next day he sank a well and to this day the clear cold spring water is flowing in abundance.

My father married Bridget White (she was always known as Bridge White - never Faley) and lived on in this house in Glasha rearing six of us. When my father fell into delicate health while he was still relatively young and had to survive on seven shillings and sixpence a week from the National Health Insurance, she did not despair. She put her shoulder to the wheel and supplemented the household budget by daily labouring out in the bogs forking and footing turf. She returned home each evening and went through the usual household duties that awaited her. She walked to Glin weekly for the provisions, handicapped with a heavy woollen shawl generally worn by women at that time. She was noted for her fast walking and there is a story told about how one day she was passing Dan Maurice Culhane's homestead on her way to Glin. Dan was pulling out of the yard with the horse and cart going in the same direction and he said to her "Would it be delaying you Ma'am if you took a lift in the car?" Yet in spite of all her demands she found time to visit and console a sick neighbour and to attend and help lay out a corpse for a wake and act as midwife to a woman in labour before hospitals were resorted to as much as they are today. She never missed Mass on a Sunday and saw to it that her children did not either, even though it meant "shanks mare " for four miles to the village of Athea. Every night the family Rosary was said as we gathered round the hearth; this was the central place in every home. We all knelt down to pray for those at home and those abroad in exile.

Upon this hearthstone the fire never died out. 'Twas raked with ashes at night. It was then still alive in the morning to be re-kindled. Many of the old people were very slow and reluctant to change over to the range. Somehow the kitchen didn't look the same anymore with the fire hidden away behind the closed doors for the flames of an open fire were like a welcoming beacon inviting everyone to come and sit near it.

I remember life at home before I reached school going age, and I remember the very first day I went to school and the other pupils who accompanied me and my brothers along the Glin road to

Ballyguiltenane in 1926. Indeed some of them have since crossed the great divide. May they rest in peace. I was nearly seven when I went to school in Ballyguiltenane, which was about three miles by road but we cut across the mountain. In summertime the boys and girls, without exception, vamped the road barefoot. All the boys wore short trousers above the knees while the girls were dressed to their ankles. The Headmaster at that time was Master Griffin and it was the custom, in order to coax children to school, to give a penny to the new pupil and two pence to the one that would bring the pupil to school. So I got a penny and my brother Bill R.I.P. got two pence.

My mother was awful strict about sending us, especially the boys, to school and even though we were the farthest from the school we always pleased the Master with our good attendance. I remember receiving a watch and chain as a reward for best attendance once, which was a great incitement to keep going. There were four teachers - Master Griffin, who was later replaced by Master Casey, Master O Grady, Miss Connolly and Miss Fahy. During our days in 1st and 2nd classes there was great importance attached to the Catechism and the Table-book. We were given lots of homework on these subjects and had all the tables - addition, subtraction, multiplication and division - learned off before third class. This was much harder than it is now as it involved the pounds, shillings and pence, halfpenny and farthing; long before the days of the metric system. For example we would say 2 multiplied by 7 = 14 = 1 shilling and 2 pence. Homework at night was more difficult also with only the dim light of a candle between three or four of us.

I left Ballyguiltenane when I was about twelve and then went on to Knocknagorna for two years, where I found that I was way ahead of the others in my class. I left school at fourteen years to go working in the bog and had no more schooling after that.

Memories of schooldays are embedded in my mind and I often recall as I travel back along boithrín na smaointe, the lessons and poems I learned off by heart. We got a great lot of this to do from our enthusiastic teacher, Mr. O Casey (R.I.P). I remember the words from the first poem in my reading book in third class and I wonder if my classmates who read this will remember it also. Those in the same class with me then, as far as I can recall, were John Fennell, Dick Normile, Paddy Mulvihill, Pat Enright, Tom Hanrahan, Mick Hanrahan, Seán Casey, Con Higgins, John Lynch, Mick Mulvihill, Paddy Sweeney, Pat Culhane, Paddy Hogan, Michael Fitz and Tom Cregan. The opening lines were:

All in an April evening
April airs were abroad
Sheep with their little lambs
Passed me by on the road
All in an April evening
I thought on the Lamb of God

Further on in its pages was another poem we got to memorise and which my mind still retains and which I am now writing from memory after having it all these years.

"My soul! There is a country
Far beyond the stars
Where stands a winged sentry
All skilful in the wars.
There above noise and danger
Sweet peace stands crowned with smiles
And One born in a manger
Commands thy beauteous files
He is thy gracious friend
And Oh! My soul awakes
Did in pure love descend
To die here for thy sake.
Leave then thy foolish ranges
For none can thee secure
But one who never changes
Thy God, thy life, thy cure."

It appeared that a lot of the poems then in the schoolbooks had a religious dimension.

We did a lot of Irish but I must admit that I have a lot of it forgotten, but the proverbs or "seanfhocail" I still retain. What I didn't know then, but later realised, was that the learning off of these "seanfhocail" was a great way of retaining the language.

To jog the memory of these classmates of mine I will write one of those stories I learned off by heart while I was in third class, as taught by Master Casey.

" I gcontae áirithe ar an dtuath bhí sé de nós aoibhinn ar na thuismitheóirí brontannas éigean a chur ar trial ar an mháistir ó am go h-am. Lá amháin labhair garsún leis an máistir, 'Gam pardún agat. Tá m'athair ag smaoineamh ar muc do mharú agus dúirt sé liom a rá leat an glacfaidh tú píosa bagún le do thoil'. 'O,' arsan Máistir, 'glacfaidh agus fáilte'. D'imigh seachtain ansin, coicís ansin, mí ar fad ach ní fhaca an máistir an muicfheóil ag teacht. 'Sea' ar seisean leis an garsún, 'ceapas go raibh píosa bacún do thabhairt liom ach níor mharaigh d'athair an muc is dócha.' 'Ó níor mharaigh, a dhuine uasal.' 'Cad ina thaobh?' 'Ó is amhlaidh atá sí leigheasta arís.'"

I remember events since I was very young indeed. One of the events that sticks in my mind is when I was taken to Glin to be inoculated against the pox, or as they used to say then "cut for the pox" when there were four little incisions made on the arm of the child vaccinated. This was done when the child was very young but I remember quite clearly kicking up a screaming scene with old Dr. Barrett as he was making me immune to smallpox.

I remember during my schooldays when April came round. Our greatest concern and desire was where would we get the price of a spinning top, even though it was only costing one old penny. These tops were always stocked at this time of year at Rice Danaher's in Athea where we made our purchase. We got many hours pleasure from these tops at school and at home. To have a successful display with our tops, the cord that we wound around it was important for it had to be the right thickness and woven in such a way that it wouldn't unravel as we wound it round and round the head of the top.

On one end of this cord was a small circular piece of leather. This was held behind the lúdeen (small finger) and the next finger to prevent the cord leaving the hand as the top left with all the force at the spinner's command. A top was like a large hen egg in shape and size, pointed at one end into where a spear was inserted.

Although all tops were of the same design and all looked alike, still a small percentage would hold spinning longer and brought fame to the owners who looked on them with pride as they kept spinning when the others had staggered and died. I have memories of our tops going to sleep as we used say - that was when the top would be spinning so smoothly and so silently that you'd hardly see it moving.

Four or five together would play a game of tops. A circle was outlined with the spear of a top on the schoolyard. Then a line was drawn fifteen feet or so from this circle for a starting point. Next a stone was placed in the circle and those taking part spun their tops as close as possible to the stone and the one farthest from the mark should place his top on the starting line.

The others should endeavour to get this top into the circle by hitting it with their top while still spinning. At times the top hit it as it left the cord. This was in order so the owner could take the spinning top from the yard by flicking it into the palm of his hand between his index and middle finger and then strike the other top on the ground and move it towards the circle.

The first one failing to strike the top with his spinning top should place his top on the ground. The owner of the idle top would take it up and play on and the game would continue like this until a top was forced into the circle. The winners would be rewarded by getting as many pecks with the spear of their tops on the head of the losers top as 'twas placed spear downwards in a firm position. The number of 'pecks' or 'handles' as we called them was stated before the game began.

The love for the tops was so great that the owners of the punished top felt as if it was himself that was suffering as the blows fell on the crown of his beloved top.

Along with the tops, in the summer months we played with marbles or 'thaws' as we called them. The procedure was much like the game with tops. A circle was made and a starting point formed a distance away. Usually two together played this game. When it was decided, after pinking the thaws to find who would go the nearest to the mark, one thaw was placed on the yard a little away from the line. His opponent would endeavour to get it into the circle by pinking his thaw with his thumb and index finger. If he failed to strike the thaw on the ground his own would take its place and thus the game would swing to and fro until a thaw entered the circle.

The winner's prize was not money like they play for today for there was no money in the pockets of the pupils then. Instead there was a string of buttons, which was held in more regard than the money of today and accepted with the same pleasure.

While the boys played with tops and thaws, the girls, sitting around in a circle played 'gobs'. Each girl picked five small pebbles, which they scattered from their hand not too separated from one another. They then picked up one, which they threw in the air. Quickly they picked up another one in time to catch the one falling. Then the two in the hand they threw overhead and picked two off the ground in time to catch the two falling. Then the four were cast up and the one remaining on the ground was picked up and the four in the air were caught before any of them hit the ground. A simple pastime but it still gave hours of pleasure to the innocent minded girls repeating the process over and over again.

I'm sure most people of my age will remember playing with a bowley. The bowley was generally a stock band - that is an iron band that was on the two edges of the stock of the banded wooden wheel of the common cart. To one who may not know I will explain that the stock was the inner part of the wheel that held the end of the twelve spokes. The other end was held in the six fellows, which formed the outer rim that was shod with a strong iron band.

We propelled our bowleys with a stick tipping them as we galloped in a race with our companions. We found fun too racing as we held a stick by one end on which a polish tin was held by a nail to its side near the other end that rolled along as we ran barefoot and carefree.

We had happy moments too as we made a purchase in our "shops" which were usually situated in a sheltered corner of the haggard beside the dwelling house. We scooped out a large cavity in a fence in which we placed shelves to hold up the goods we sold and it was decorated with "chaneys" of every shape and colour got from broken delph. We sold tea and sugar and all the other items to be found in a grocer's shop. I'm afraid our goods wouldn't live up to the quality demanded today! The tea came from the dry turf dust and the sugar from the dry dust of the fence. The money exchanged was stone pebbles from the gravelled yard. Our shopkeepers were known as Mrs Cake and Mrs Chewit!

As we sat on a fence on a July evening we listened to the corncrake as we watched black clouds rolling across the sky in all their curious shapes of animals, huge forms of men and every shape of object imaginable.

At home on winter nights with my brothers and sister and cousins we played simple games that my father and other members of his family joined in when they were children back in the 1870's. My father, letting his mind drift back to his childhood days, gave us the greatest pleasure sharing his past with us. For example he would take a little splinter of bog deal and after lighting it pass it on from one to one sitting round the hearth in front of the blazing turf fire. Each one, whilst holding it, should say "Jack is alive and alive is he still. If he dies in my arms what must I give?" The person holding it as the light went out would have to forfeit something. There would be a great urgency to pass it on as it was about to quench and a great reluctance on the one to accept it for fear he'd be the one to have to pay the penalty.

Another game in much the same manner was the passing of a ring from one to one. The ring was enclosed between the palms of the hands held in the manner joined as if one was praying and the ring dropped into the other hands held in the same way as the giver went from one to one in the fireside circle. Any of the others didn't know into whose hands the ring was dropped and had to guess where it lay.

There was a little rhyme accompanying every game and in this instance the holder of the ring would chant
"Poor paw Paddy's pen
Open the door and let me in
For the sake of this gold ring."

Another game we played was "Fool in the Middle". One person stood in the middle of the kitchen floor while one stood at each of the four corners. The challenge was to exchange corners with one another without the fool in the middle getting into the corner vacated. If he did, the one dispossessed should take the place of the Fool in the middle.

Riddles had a place in many a session. Many of them were in the form of a rhyme; the answer was generally a household utensil but the riddle gave it as a living thing e.g. "Long legs, crooked thighs, small head and no eyes". The Tongs was the answer (a long instrument used for shaping up the fire and placing coals on the hearth for the griddle and on the oven cover for baking bread or roasting fowl). "Bowlegged father, fatbellied mother, three little children all one colour" Answer - The Pothooks and pot with three legs. "As round as a ring, as flat as a pan with half of a woman and the whole of a man". Answer - The old penny.

One incident, which comes to mind now, may be of interest. Back in the very early 20's it looked as if Rebel marching bands were forbidden and their musical instruments would be confiscated if found. At that time there was a band in Athea and, so that their gear would not be discovered, Paddy the Painter Liston, a man bearing a patriots heart, brought all the instruments to our very remote home in the mountains of Glasha. I heard my father tell how he hid them in a rick of turf so that the Authorities would be expected to make a very thorough search to succeed in finding them.

The instruments included all the necessary items - Drum, Kettle, Cymbals, etc. Anyway there they remained for years after until the members of the band fell apart and lost all interest and my father learned they were not to be taken back anymore. It is most surprising that anyone didn't understand the value of those musical instruments so the sad finish of them was that we children used them as playthings and they were destroyed and lost. This was much to my regret when I later realised how valuable they were; they could be of use to another band, which was formed later, in commemoration of the great Paddy Dalton of Athea, who gave his life with his comrades at Gortaglanna and is commemorated in the song "The Valleys of Knockanure".

One of my most treasured memories from childhood is listening to all the stories related by my father to us in the old traditional style of the seanchaí of which he had a great many, of fairies, ghosts, giants, and leprechauns. Although he would not have made his way up in the charts with his songs he gave us more pleasure listening to him sing and play the Jews harp than it did listening to the great Count John McCormack. He sang for us patriotic songs, love songs, comic songs and other very old songs that I've only heard the great sean nós singer Con Greaney sing. One of them was entitled "Mind your eye". "Rooska Hill", "The Colleen Deas", and the "Colleen Bawn" were other songs he gave voice to and held us spellbound. I can't remember anyone singing the "Colleen Bawn" today. I may as well pen a verse or two as I first heard it almost 80 years ago.

In the golden vales of Limerick
Where flows the Shannon stream,
There a maiden dwells who holds my heart
And haunts me like a dream.
With shining showers of golden hair
As gentle as a fawn
I was but a labouring boy
And she the Colleen Bán.

Her skin was whiter than the snow
That falls on the mountainside
And softer than the creamy foam
That floats all in the tide.
Her eye was brighter than the star
That twinkles o'er the lawn
And her cheeks would make the red nose pale
My darling Colleen Bán.

Although she seldom speaks to me
I think on her with pride
I told her how I loved her
And asked her for my bride.
Through dreary times and cold neglect
From me she has withdrawn
She is the breaking of my heart
My darling Colleen Bán.

Back in my childhood days it was customary to borrow from a neighbour if you were temporarily caught short. It might be tea or sugar or a gallon of milk for bread-making or a tin-can of flour or meal. There was never any resentment towards the borrower, as the borrowed item would always be returned. There was great co-operation between neighbours then. If a garsún was sent for a message to a neighbour's house he was bound to receive a cut of buttered bread, maybe a bit of jam on it also, but even without the jam the neighbour's bread had a flavour all of its own. It is a peculiar fact that home-made bread, made

The iron was flat and would have been placed against the hot coals until sufficiently hot to smooth out all the wrinkles. This took some time, as the iron had to be heated several times during the process. Then came the box iron which speeded up the job considerably as an iron could be placed in the centre of the fire until it was red hot, removed and then placed into the box iron. While one was working with this another iron was heating in the fire so that there was no cessation or slowing down of operations. Of course the electricity changed all this in later years.

I remember as a lad running across the fields to the "Coopers Shop" as it was called. Here Hannie Casey sold goods of all things necessary in the every day running of the home. To me then the most enticing was ten papered toffee sweets (with the manufacturers name Geary or Cleeve printed on the wrapping paper) for one old penny. I would be delighted to get the cardboard box, which contained the sweets, to cover my schoolbooks for extra protection.

I would also buy a half quarter of Plug or Bendigo tobacco, one shilling and three old pence (5c now) for my father. That was his weekly smoking requirements while I got a half-ounce of Clarke's white cap snuff costing five old pence for my mother's pleasure. I can see the delight on my father's face as he reached for his tobacco on my return from the shop and I watched with interest as he took the sharp penknife from his waistcoat pocket. He held the half quarter between the thumb and the finger of the left hand, then pared with the blade thin little layers off one end until he had enough to fill the head of the pipe. He held these shavings in the palm of his left hand and replaced the remainder of the tobacco in a little pouch before putting it into his waistcoat pocket. From another pocket he took his pipe but not before he rolled the filling of it between both palms and I watched him roll it round and round making sure that the least bit didn't get lost. Running a finger of the right hand between the fingers of the left retrieved any little bit that escaped from the palm between the fingers. The finger next to the luidín of the rights hand was always used in this process. Why, you may like to know?

The reason was that the knife with which he cut the tobacco was still held in the right hand like you'd hold a pen during the operation of grinding the tobacco. The knife had more work to do yet: after taking the pipe from his pocket he took it by the stem and tapped the cover down on his closed fist holding the cut tobacco; then he removed the cover with the remaining dust from the last smoke he had taken. He then scraped the inside with the small blade of his horn-handled knife and discarded that dust. With the index finger of the right hand he moved the cut tobacco on his left hand into a neat little pile, placed the pipe under it, held it there by his luidín and then packed it into his pipe and placed the dust which the cover contained on top. He ignited it with a lighted splinter of bog deal taken from the fire he was sitting beside and sent rings of smoke ascending to the black rafters of the kitchen as his face lit up with pleasure.

My mother found the same pleasure in freeing her nose and head with a pinch of snuff as she stitched a patch on one of our torn pants or coats and we could hear her pray "God Bless us " after each sneeze.

I remember the joy we found on rising up about eight o clock on a summers morning to hear the mowers whetting the blades with the scythe stones on the nearby meadow; the sound it made brought music to our ears and we watched with delight to see four of them bending to their work as they swung their scythes with ease and perfect rhythm, each clearing a sward of eight or nine feet and leaving the cut hay in lovely rows behind them.

Even more joy awaited me to hear that George Lynch was coming with horses and mowing machine to cut down his meadow just beside our house. We hurried home from school to behold the beautiful sight of the two horses stepping it out together with the long shaft of the machine stretching between them to which they were harnessed with traces and quins. I don't know how they became to be named thus but they were fashioned from a length of wood. One quin of three feet or so was held in the centre, hooked to the top of the shaft of the long beam of the machine and the ends attached to the collar of the horse on each side. Two traces attached to the crooks of the hames on the horses' collar were attached to another quin and those two quins were attached by the centre to the ends of a giant quin attached to the body of the machine.

On a seat on the machine George sat with a long reins to the mouth-pieces on the horses' winkers with which he kept the horses in control. He also held a long whip to spur on a horse that might be leaving more than his share of the work to his team-mate. On occa-sions like this we'd hear George's voice above the noise of the machine, shouting, "Go on there, Fanny" or " Go on Tom." Each horse understood his own name.

A very pleasant sound to my ears then was the musical notes the click-ing ratchet wheel of the machine made when it was turned out of gear when reversing to get lined up at the end of a sward changing course at right angles. I watched with interest as George placed one of the long knives of the machine over a tub of water as he sharpened each v-shaped section of the blade with a stone.

Work on the farm in those days was slow and difficult and required great skill in the planting and saving of crops. Men were proud of their expertise and working ability and willing and able to work. "He's a great man at the spade" or " He's a great man to mow" or "He's a great warrant to fill a load of hay" were remarks that were often passed.

Filling a load of hay was not as simple as it sounds. First the wheels overhead the body of the cart had to be protected from the hay; this was done by placing a shield called a guard on both sides of the cart with its legs protruding down between the sidelace and the shaft. One man stood on the wynd to fork the hay up to the man in the cart who had to carefully roll it when placing it on the rider as he filled up the four corners. He started at the back of the cart, placed a roll on the right and left rider and then fashioned a smaller roll to hold those in place. Over this he placed a fork of unrolled hay and continued to work at the front in the same order. Each layer extended out beyond the one underneath so that when the load was finished it was extending back and forth far beyond the confines of the cart; otherwise you were in trouble, as the cart would capsize if the wheel went into a rut. There were men who could fit a ton of hay upon a cart, which was considered a very large amount. In a well-filled load the animal bearing the cart would eat from the front of the load.

Generally the farmers "cored" with each other bringing the hay from the meadows to be stacked beside the cowhouse for the winter fodder, so it was customary to see a meitheal (crowd) in the farmyard on such an occasion. The weather was always a worry and every eye scanned the sky before work was started as 'twould never do to have a large stack of hay half made when rain would come pouring down. So it had to be absolutely certain that the day would remain dry before the stack would be laid out.

In later years the haybarn removed the worry of the weather for if the day rained the work could come to halt without fear of damage to the hay in the barn. The hayfloat came next which removed the forking of hay from wynd to cart as the wynd was drawn in by a rope with the aid of a wheel at the side of the float. This was a great boon at the time but was made very remote when the tractors and rotomowers and cocklifters and front loaders came along. It is very few wynds of hay that are seen now as farmers have turned over to baled hay and silage.

One of the chores which children undertook in their school hours was picking thistles and "costavaun" and nettles. I remember well going off to the neighbouring fields with a bag and with my hands guarded with a stocking pulled over them I inserted the blade of the knife under the thistle, cut the stem and transferred it into the bag that previously held ten stone of meal. I continued on until I had the bag full, packing it down occasionally with my foot, then hoisting it on my back I brought it home. It was then placed in a wooden container where it was cut into very small particles with a cutter. It was then mixed with yellow meal and fed to the poultry, which were kept by every housewife.

The cutter was a blade six inches or so long, fashioned by the blacksmith in his forge, much like the present day hoe but the holder on the blade was only one foot long. It could be held when cutting in one or both hands.

* * *

"Will you take these shoes into the shoemaker to half sole them. He might do them while you're waiting to get confession." Thus my mother spoke to me one Saturday as I was starting out for Athea. That was at the time when confession always preceded our reception of Holy Communion. We would never go to the rails in the Church unless we had been to Confession the day before and we would make sure we had not partaken of any food since midnight the previous night. This was in the days when we walked or cycled to Mass.

Anyway I took the shoes into Connie Cahill who was shoemaker and repairer then. He later went on to become postman. As a young lad I was fascinated to watch Connie at work. At that time the work of a shoe repairer or cobbler as they were called was an indispensable social service in Ireland.

The Cobbler's shop was generally small with one small window, which you'd think would not afford much light for the man to work. Generally the door was open - maybe to give extra light. There always appeared to be a great lot of work ahead of the cobbler for the shelves were full of shoes for repairs, some of them beyond repair but he wouldn't have the heart to tell customers that and they were left there to gather dust until eventually the owner himself forgot about them.

Usually the small workbench is covered with tools and half-repaired shoes - the last and the hammer having pride of place. There is no place for customers to sit; there is just one chair and the cobbler has that. The hammer is light and he taps it ever so gently in quick succession. As I said earlier I found great pleasure looking at Connie fill his mouth with tacks, dispense them with his lips and tap them home with the hammer as he bound on the half-sole. First he soaked it in water to soften it. Then he cut it into the shape of the sole with a razor-sharp knife. He then tapped it with his hammer to make it more pliable. After laying it in position and sinking an impression around the perimeter for the course of the tack, he rapidly tapped them on.

In some cases the sole was bound on by sewing especially if the shoe was of a high quality and the leather thin. In this case the wax end had to be made. This was done with three or four threads of wax hemp being twisted by the skilled hand of the cobbler over his knee, next the hemp was waxed and a rub of soap made it slippery for working through the holes made by the awl. Sewing with a wax end was a slow process; one end had to be passed through each hole, the other end was hitched to it and both ends were pulled tight to form each stitch.

There were strong boots too with hobnailed soles and steel tips. These could be heard echoing as a man walked the flagged footpaths in the town and it might be company for a man walking home alone in the dark. However a man wouldn't get much pleasure from it if he was walking up the chapel, late for mass, especially if the tip was loose!

The last pair of hobnailed boots that I wore with tips on them I gave to my nephew Denny Falahee when he was anchorman in a tug-of-war team in Ardagh. I'm sure they helped in his team winning!

The wellington and rubber boots have replaced the hobnailed ones; they are more waterproof than the leather. Still the hobnails were a great relief to the labourer to drive home the treadle of a spade or sleán and many were the goals that were scored with them by robust men on the football field. Yes, indeed, many was the mile of road covered to fairs and markets as they sounded loud and clear along the roadway on a frosty morning.

* * *

A short distance east of Blaine Cross on the Kerry line lived James Lynch. James was a Cooper by trade and at that time before the advent of the Creamery a cooper's trade was a thriving business. He made barrels, firkins, pecks and all other timber utensils connected with the making of butter.

When the milking was done the milk was strained and lodged in large pans or timber 'pecks' and placed in the dairy. The dairy was an out-house or a room attached to the dwelling house with a stand or long bench on which the pecks or pans rested. Long after the change over to the creamery those houses were referred to as "The Dairy" although they were no longer used as such.

After the milk lodging for a day or two the cream that formed on top was skimmed off by a skimmer, which was a kind of large spoon, and put into a cream tub. When after some days enough cream was collected for butter making the cream was put into a churn. This churn was a timber barrel with a cover. Inside the barrel was a churnstaff which was a circular piece of wood with four holes around the edge and a long handle in the centre which came upwards through a hole in the centre of the cover. Lifting up and pounding down this churnstaff time and time again until the butter was made. At the beginning this was pounded in rapid succession but as the butter was forming it was used more slowly. In the finish the butter collected all together in one lump surrounded by the buttermilk. It was then removed from the churn with a timber spade washed repeatedly in cold water until it was quite clean after being turned over and over with the butter spades. It was then salted and packed into firkins for the market in Listowel, which was the market town for the locality.

The buttermilk was used to make bread. It was also used as a drink and there was nothing so satisfying to quench the thirst as a mug of buttermilk! A pointer of mixed bread baked on the griddle and a mug of buttermilk made a very palatable meal. "It would grow hair on your chest" they used to say. Of course, the buttermilk was also used to feed calves, pigs and bonhams.

To get back to the Cooper's Shop, it was a landmark on the Kerryline. A stranger making enquiries for a certain destination would be told

"It's the next house beyond the Coopers" or the second or third as the case may be.

James Lynch, the cooper, married Hannie Casey who outlived him for many years. She opened a shop here in which she sold all kinds of everything and carried on a thriving business. She served the needs of the people of Glenagragra, Drumreask, Ballyguiltenane and Dirreen. The customers at that time came mostly on shanks mare and there were paths across shortcuts from the Glin road and from Drumreask and Scart to Hannie's shop. This house was also the rendezvous for card players and many is the game of "41" that was singled out there with the best of gamblers. The stakes at that time were usually a halfpenny each game.

Here too the young lads and ladies went night-walking for there was always a welcome for everyone as Hannie, God rest her, was the kindest, most affectionate and generous hearted woman. She was very concerned in bringing courting couples together and many is the date that was arranged for the Coopers. I'm sure many of the couples that were married in townlands round about were after spending some nights in the Coopers shed! This shed was across the road from the shop. In it Hannie kept her cow and in part of it was stored some hay and fodder. Into this shed romantic couples retreated in the wintertime. In summertime the lovers sought a quiet spot in the corner of a meadow by the roadside. As the seanchaí used to say the daisies came in for a bit of flattening. There was one snag in the open air courting as it was very hard to avoid the tell-tale snail tracts on one's clothes after coming in contact with the grass. There were no lounge bars or motorcars then so Hannie's shed provided protection against the elements when winter set in. At night when Hannie would take a flashlamp to see her cow, as she was wont to do before retiring, she might often find lovers caressing in the shed but she'd just say in her gentle way "Don't forget when ye are leaving to shut the door and throw a sop to the cow."

Another rendezvous for the neighbouring boys and girls in the late 40's and early 50's was Maurice Higgins house in Glasha. Many is the happy night we spent around the big turf fire in the open hearth. The kitchen was a large farmhouse type so that there was ample room for the large circle which attended there night after night where a "céad mile fáilte" (one hundred thousand welcomes) was extended to everyone.

This was before the advent of lounge bars and ballad sessions when local entertainment consisted of a weekly dance at Behane's Hall in Knockdown where the admission was only four old pence. The hall used to be packed to the door even though most of the people came on foot as during the war years it was next to impossible to find a bicycle or parts to keep one in order. At that time too the Church forbade any dancing during the season of Lent and all dance hall owners strictly observed this order. Instead there were the travelling shows which were a great attraction and provided good entertainment. Thus the idea that we could have our own shows and travel out with them was conceived in the minds of a few comrades of an adventurous nature that formed the circle of Higgins. After nursing the idea for a while and getting others interested a copy of a three act play "A Will and a Woman" was obtained and the "Gragra Dramatic Class" was born. Curiously, all of the company resorting in this Rambling house were members of the Pioneer Association and were welded together under that banner. The dramatic class grew to be a great success and the plays were accompanied by music, song and dance supplied by our own gathering of neighbours. We performed in all the local villages in West Limerick from Ballysteen to Asdee, from Glin to Tournafulla. The proceeds were spent each year in financing a tour of Kerry for the group members, which we all enjoyed very much. We can look back now with pleasant memories on the fun and good sport we had together producing our plays in that happy atmosphere in the warm cosy home in Higgins's.

A Welcome to Glenbawn

Come all welcome tourists who visit our Isle
Come here to West Limerick 'twill be worth your while
Whenever you call be it nightfall or dawn
There's something of beauty to be seen in Glenbawn.

When you touch down at Shannon come to the city
Then on for Askeaton by the docks there you'll see
From there to Shanagolden by the Stonecutter's lawn
Turn left, then you're right on the road to Glenbawn.

When you come to the Moig Cross there you'll see a road sign
Then turn to your right by the sweet Carnagh Line
Keep on straight ahead 'til you'll cross the Abha Bhan
That's fed with the streamlets flowing down from Glenbawn.

From the top of Glenbawn what a wonderful scene
The blue purple mountains and valleys so green
Far over the Shannon down by Fairylawn
The beauties of nature can be seen from Glenbawn.

To the East, famed Knockpatrick stands guard o'er the plain
Commanding a view of the rich Golden Vein
To the West, Cnoc an Óir keeps a look out at dawn
To see the sun rising o'er lovely Glenbawn.

If you are a sportsman and handle the gun
With the woodcock and pheasant 'tis there you'll have fun
You'll see the grouse rising from the white canavaun
And the snipe shoot like rockets from the springs of Glenbawn.

Perhaps you're an angler and anxious to fish
Then bring on your tackle, you can have your wish
With your rod and line on the banks of the Abha Bhán
Or in Clounleharde river that flows by Glenbawn.

If you want to go dancing we have colleens go leór
And boys for the maidens who visit our shore
The grand Irish Ceili they'll dance until dawn
As they stamp on the floor around lovely Glenbawn.

An Exile's Dream

Oh purling little stream you are ever in my dream,
Since lonely I did part with you one day,
Yet I see each twist and turn and with love my heart did burn,
For my home in dear old Glenbawn far away.

There along your banks we wandered when our childhood days we
squandered,
As we listened to the skylark's lovely lay,
And the blackbirds and thrushes piped forth from the bushes,
Round my home in dear old Glenbawn far away.

The wild flowers there we gathered
that along the banks were scattered,
As we heard the cuckoo calling all the May,
And with bare feet together we roamed the fields and heather,
Round my home in dear old Glenbawn far away.

Our fond comrades we'd be meeting
to exchange the kindly greeting,
When we met there at the crossroads with our spirits gay,
As the fiddles would be ringing and
sweet songs we would be singing,
Near my home in dear old Glenbawn far away.

Now here in this rich land of dollars
away from the "saints and scholars",
Each morning noon and night I'll always pray,
Whilst there's life in limb and liver
to go back to that dear river,
And my home in dear old Glenbawn far away.
But if God should so command it that my life

He will demand it,
And my body in a foreign land will stay,
Oh that my soul may pass in transit
from this world to that beyond it,
Through my home in dear old Glenbawn far away.

On the Death of my Wife

The cold hand of death has us severed
And I am left here brokenhearted
Us two so endeared and united
Nothing but death could have parted
There 'was one thing even death failed to conquer
Though the life from your limbs it wiped out
The smile ever part of your features
Was there as you lay wrapped in the shroud.

Your willing hands were always extended
To help strangers and kin and kith
You were a bright ray of sunshine
To everyone you made contact with
Your many friends most sincerely
Come to offer their deep sympathy
But no words can extinguish the sorrow
That's choking the life out of me.
What a loss you are to your children
They're too young to shed many tears
But they'll miss their fond mother's guidance

Happy days in Glasha

In Glasha I was happy upon my father's knee,
As he sang and told us stories that filled our hearts with glee,
The giants and ghosts and leprechauns are still clear in my mind,
That I heard of long ago in innocent happy times.

In Glasha I was happy as off to school we ran,
With our feet bare and toughened and on our cheeks a tan,
All through the long hot summer days with playmates all together,
Oh, how good 'twould be if God ordained those days should last for-
ever.

In Glasha I was happy when Christmas came around,
And lots of nice things to eat on the table would be found,
Before Christmas we'd do nothing wrong and were very good
because,
Otherwise we'd not receive a thing from Santa Claus.

In Glasha I was happy when I heard the cuckoo's voice,
In clear and mellow tones our spirit to rejoice,
There upon the treetop as the bright sun did shine,
Her notes rang out in harmony along the Kerryline.

In Glasha I was happy to ride on the load of hay,
As 'twas carted from the meadow to the haggard there to lay,
Until 'twas forked into the big stack when the meitheal came,
They were all enjoying their work accomplishing that same.

In Glasha I was happy in our local football team,
As we challenged Knocknagorna, Ballyguiltenane and Dirreen,

We thought we were all champions then like Mick O'Connell in his
day,
Hoping to win the Sam Maguire with the boys of Behane's Raye.

In Glasha I was happy when the shades of nights did fall,
And we all congregated in Tom Behane's dance hall,
And there what entertainment with spirits soaring high,
And many a couple met that later in marriage bed did lie.

In Glasha I was happy when our Dramatic Class was formed,
And in the surrounding towns on the stage we did perform,
We always did enjoy the craic as we travelled in Jack's lorry,
Huddled in together without a care or worry.

In Glasha I was happy with thick ice on the pond,
Skating with our hobnailed boots as we went hand in hand,
Speeding along down in our 'grug' or balancing on one foot,
We often took a tumble but didn't care a hoot.

In Glasha I was happy when on my pedal bike,
When with my companions to Ballybunion we did hike,
Crowds of neighbouring boys and girls on their bikes would feel so
gay,
And no journey on a Sunday was ever too far away.

In Glasha I was happy when we were hunting the wren,
And surely did enjoy the night when the wren dance came on,
God be with the good old days and the great craic we had,
In homes of Paddy Flavin, Maurice Higgins and Langan Pat.

The Life and Rhymes of Paddy Faley

In Glasha I was happy when hare hunting we would go,
On Sunday after Mass we searched high and low,
How excited we became when the brown hare did appear,
And the shouts of hull-a-hull rang out loud and clear.

In Glasha I was happy when early in the Spring,
Our sharpened spades and bags of scioláns to the gardens we would
bring,
There in ridges long and straight we turned the taibhóids,
To produce the harvest crop we took home in loads.

In Glasha I was happy when mild April did dawn,
As we set out for the bog with barrow, fork and sleán,
There to our heart's contentment we worked hard each day,
As the long spread of turf on the sward behind us lay.

In Glasha I was happy when the turf ricks long and high,
Were clamped on the roadside for the market by and by,
Then from the rich takings we could cut a dash,
Where there was no inflation and our pockets full of cash.

In Glasha I was happy when with my whetted blade,
I swung through fields of corn and meadows low I laid,
For my youthful muscles then feared not shovel, spade or scythe,
And the harder the work was the more I did enjoy it.

In Glasha I was happy putting on a roof of thatch,
With the straw and scallops that no other roof could match,
'Twas so warm in the Winter and in Summer kept us cool,
With sparrows nesting 'neath its eaves, said to be lucky as a rule.

In Glasha I was happy when a flood was in the Gale,
With fishing rod and line we along its banks did trail,
There in the many currents the big trout took the bait,
And thrilling were the stories the anglers did relate.

In Glasha I was happy when Winter nights came on,
As we sat around the table in a game of 41,
When the opposition was 36 what pleasure to me it gave,
To hold within my hand the ace and five and knave.

In Glasha I was happy when I brought my blushing bride,
And heard her merry laughter ringing o'er the mountainside,
We knew not a dull moment, it looks as if time stands still,
For often in my reverie I hear her laughter's thrill.

Now in my old days I am happy with armchair and book,
As through the local journals I with interest doth look,
And there read something that recalls the good times I went through,
To relive again the memories of good friends fond and true.

Killing the Pig

Every family produced its own bacon and it was customary to kill a pig as the stock of meat ran out. The killing of the pig was a ceremonious event. Preparations had to be made. The people in rural areas believed that the moon controlled more on earth than the tides and when arranging a date to kill it had to be, if at all possible, when the moon was waxing; they held the belief that the meat from the pig at that time would be of better quality and would swell in the boil whereas it was quite the contrary if the killing took place with the waning moon.

So a date was arranged with a man possessing the skill and ability of performing such a task; such men were rare and since so many pigs were being killed he was kept busy so he had to be notified well in advance. On the morning of the appointed day, large pots of water were boiled, a big firm table procured and the help of three or four neighbours requested, but this was no problem as the neighbours were always eager and willing to co-operate in helping each other out. When the butcher, as we may call him, arrived, the pig was brought into the kitchen. The woman of the house sprinkled the holy water (in those times the sprinkling of the holy water and the asking of God's blessings on the work preceded every important event). A rope was fastened in the pig's mouth with the man holding it standing directly in front. The butcher stood on the left of the pig and held a spear against the pig's forehead. This spear was specially made for the occasion. The spear was about four inches long with a handle two feet. The butcher held the handle as a man with muscular arms, standing on the right hand side, drove the spear with a heavy mallet. The pig collapsed immediately. It was then lifted on to a table and placed on its back. The neck was washed clean. Now the butcher inserted a large meat knife through the pig's neck in front of the chest. It was then quickly turned on its side so the woman of the house was ready with the bread pan or other large container to receive the blood which had gushed forth through the incision made by the knife which was still inserted in the throat. The pig was laid on one side of the table and boiling water was poured over the body to remove the hair, which became loose and could be scraped off with a knife. The cleaning continued first one side then on the other until every bit of hair was removed and the skin was shining. The body was then hung up, the hind legs tied to the end of a rafter or a ladder placed upright against a wall. The body was then opened by cutting straight down the entire length of the front and the heart, liver, stomach and intestines taken out and the body was left hanging overnight. As a child I remember the excitement of blowing up the bladder and tying a knot in it to make a football.

After the pig had been hanging in the gallows overnight the butcher came again to cut it down. First the head was removed, next the backbone thus cutting the body in two halves. Each half was cut into four or five pieces according to the size of the pig. From each piece the bones were removed together with any surplus of lean meat which was called pork steak.

The timber barrel was now placed in position with a few light strips of wood placed inside at the bottom so that the pickle, when it formed, could penetrate the meat. The skin was pierced with a sharp knife, each slit a few inches apart. On to this was rubbed a generous quantity of salt. The rubbing continued for a considerable time before the meat was placed in the barrel, each piece on top of the other with a thin layer of salt in between. A large stone was placed on top and there the meat rested to cure undisturbed for three weeks. It was then taken out and hung on the meatstick, which was a beam of wood nailed to the rafters, generally over the fire, with a crook for each piece to be used when required.

While the men were salting the meat the woman of the house, with the help of a few neighbours, was busy making puddings. The first step was to clean all the intestines or guts which had been turned inside out under running water. When they had been scraped clean and transparent they were cut into lengths and one end tied with a cord. The pig's blood, which had been collected the day before, now formed the basis of the puddings. Into this was added oatmeal, onions, bread-crumbs, milk, grated portions of the boiled heart and liver, pepper and salt. The woman would taste the raw mixture to make sure it had enough of all ingredients. This mixture was inserted into the intestine which was held in the left hand while being filled with the fingers of the right hand. Leaving a few inches for expansion the two ends were tied securely making the pudding into a ring ready to be cooked in a pot of very hot but not boiling water. After simmering for a certain time the rings were removed and placed to cool by hanging on to the handle of a brush which was balanced between two chairs.

The custom then was to send a portion of the first pork steak and a pudding to all the neighbours in the townland. There were various comments on the flavour and quality of the black pudding and one often heard the remark "She is a great warrant to fill a pudding."

Threshing the Corn

The ground for the corn was usually that from which a crop of potatoes had been produced. It was ploughed with horses and the corn
covered with a harrow drawn by horses. The corn was cut with a reaping hook in those far off days and perhaps not so far off as there are
men whom I know who tell me they used the reaping hook to cut
wheat.

The corn was bound in sheaves built in "stooks" and later was taken
from the garden and stacked in the "haggard". Later in the year when
the harvesting was over, the corn was threshed. This as I have said
already took place in the kitchen. Usually a dry frosty day was cho-
sen for the work. The corn was placed in two rows the length of the
floor with the grain ends placed meeting each other. A flail was used
for this purpose.

The flail consisted of a length of wood -four feet approximately -
made of ash or such tough material bound on to the end of another
piece of similar length by a leather thong. A man holding one piece in
both hands, swung the flail over his shoulder bringing it down hard on
top of the grain, thereby separating the grain from the stem. He
worked along the row, from one end to the other and when one lot was
threshed he removed the straw and replaced it with another lot. The
chaff was winnowed from the grain by letting both fall onto a sheet in
the open on a breezy day, the breeze blowing the chaff away.

The grain was then filled into bags and stored for feeding horses and
poultry. The straw was used for bedding and thatch. The straw also
contributed to the making of the bed mattress. At the time, the maize
meal or "Yalla Male" as it was called came in bags weighing twenty
stones and it was no more bother at the time for a man to heave it onto
his back to remove it to or from the cart. From those bags was made
a large bag, the size of the bed. It was then stuffed with the straw and
placed on the bed with a feather tick laid over it, comfortable enough,

but it had one disadvantage - it was the breeding ground for fleas and them were the lively "buckos". No sooner had a person stretched himself on the bed than they were dancing rock and roll across his chest and if a stranger lodged in the house they declared war on him with a vengeance.

The most annoying thing of all was when a flea entered the confines of the ear; that was the tatarara he created. There was no way of getting him out only to get out of the bed, probe your way in the darkness to the kitchen, scoop in the drawer of the table for a spoon and risk hitting your toes or shin against the skillet and pots at the butt of the kitchen as you sought your way to the bucket of spring water that reposed in the bottom of the dresser. Then, taking a spoon of the water and tilting the head sideways, you poured it into your ear to flood out the invader.

The yellow meal mentioned above, was used both for human consumption and animal use and the old people believed there was nothing better to fatten pigs.

Irish Homes of Long Ago

Before we heard the wireless or the television we did watch,
We sat cosily round the fire beneath our roof of thatch,
As we heard the fairy stories told, entertaining old and young,
And our hearts were filled with rapture as we heard the old songs
sung,
As the flames from the big turf fire set the house aglow,
There was a little bit of heaven in the Irish homes of long ago.

The cricket from the hob sang out as if in the fun to join,
The dog would gaze and seem to smile beside the fireside lying,
The music from the fiddle chased all our cares away,
And the piper's lively tuning made every heart feel gay,
As there upon the flagstone we tapped it, heel and toe,
In a lively reel or polka in the Irish homes of long ago.

In innocent simple pastimes young and old would take part,
And their loud joyous laughter would raise the cockles of your
heart,
While the housewife with her needles did busily knit and sew,
As she enjoyed the merriment in the Irish homes of long ago.

The wholesome conversation was of interest to all,
As local matters were discussed and problems big and small,
They thrashed out relations 'til no one had any doubts,
Of whose blood they inherited from their ancestral roots,
Always ready to help each other in any grief or woe,
The true spirit of God was in 'em in the Irish homes of long ago.

Before the advent of machinery the labourer won praise,
For his skill and endurance in the long hour working days,
They enjoyed their work with scythe and spade and returned thanks
to God,

For his blessings on their homesteads and big families they had,
And there upon their knees at night to Heaven their prayers would go,
As the Rosary they recited in the Irish homes of long ago.

Ballyguiltenane School 1956

Come all you gay people in search of good sport
Come to the schoolhouse it's the latest resort
And join in the hooley that now has begun
With the clergy of Glin in Ballyguiltenane

The place was unheard of 'til a few months ago
The priests then decided to bring on this show
And wake up the spirits in woman and man
And make life worth living in Ballyguiltenane

Now they come there in hundreds from miles all around
From Glin and Athea, Listowel and Newtown
They come in lorries, in hackneys and vans
Form Tarbert and Tarmons to Ballyguiltenane

Try living with Lynch and take the floor with Din Joe
Or tune into Lux in your old radio
But the best that you hear is like a fry in a pan
Compared to the racket in Ballyguiltenane

Sure there is nothing but gaiety filling the air
No talk of the budget or the rates you'll hear there
Old pensioners dancing like they were twenty-one
They found Tir na nÓg in Ballyguiltenane

For a paltry few bob there you get a treat
Of music and song and a supper to eat
A dance and a card drive of the old '41'
And a pound for the winner in Ballyguiltenane

Ye men that are single, come now is your chance
You'll get a life partner if you come to this dance
And enjoy the comfort that God made for man
He wants no bachelors at all in Ballyguiltenane

To the women I say give up sleeping alone
With jars of hot-water to heat up your bones
Come here to our schoolhouse and you'll get a man
That will swell you with heat in Ballyguiltenane

To the clergy up in Glin sure great credit is due
God bless and protect them their equals are few
For there every Sunday since winter began
There's mass and confessions in Ballyguiltenane

It's a great boon for the people so far from the town
Signs by their dear clergy they will not let him down
They are eager to help any scheme they bring on
And support their great project in Ballyguiltenane

For years in Glin district they gave the doctor no rest
With pains in their bones and they sadly depressed
But now they're all bouncing their arthritis is gone
They found the right doctor in Ballyguiltenane.

Knocknagorna School
To my old school pal Jim O'Sullivan

Many moons have waxed and waned

and there are changes by the score

Since first you left your homeland to seek a foreign shore

But you're still fresh in my memory as

when we sat together on the long stool

With our teacher Mr Kenny in Knocknagorna school

I'm certain that your mind like mine sometimes travels back

Along the road of memory along our childhood track

As barefoot we went romping with

our books and lunch and rule

All happy, gay and carefree to Knocknagorna school.

Ah! Those were the happy days that we'll never see again

When we climbed for hazel nuts down in Mullane's Glen

Or a football game contested in the field below the road

And quenched our thirst from the spring well

near Tom John's abode.

Knockadullaun Winter 1959

Alas I am sorry this story to state
About poor misfortunes that depend on the State
They're called from the dole to make a bog road
So that turf can come out by the big lorry load
On the top of a mountain near reaching the sky
From the bed of the river 'tis 800-feet high
And the cold that is there it would perish a sleán
So God help the poor workmen in Knockadullaun.

Their hours they are long and the work is severe
In the cold frosty days at this time of the year
And it's a crying shame in a country like ours
To give them for dinner a single half hour
With no time to go in from the hailstones and snow
But eat in the open like the slaves long ago
We thought freedom's day in this country did dawn
It doesn't look like that in Knockadullaun.

Inside a wet ditch like the poor refugees
With a sup of cold tay our insides to freeze
No wonder our people are getting thinned out
'Tis this kind of cruelty that brings it about
For you know what will happen from drinking cold tay
'Twill stretch the whole lot of us in Templeathea
But 'tis the Government's way to stop the dole we are drawin'
To freeze us to death there in Knockadullaun.

They say all these rules are laid down in the Dail
Where there's no consideration for labourers at all
They say they're a burden on the ratepayer and tax
Too lazy to work or to bend down their backs
But they'll give big grants to farmers the water to run
And before they'd pay labour they'd leave it undone

The Ministers don't care, big salaries they're drawin'
We can live on fresh air around Knockadullaun.

Our famous Frank Aiken is spouting abroad
About the cruel doings of Mr. Kruschev the fraud
He'll show 'em how to stop the Russian advance
He'll remove the Iron Curtain if he'll have a chance
He can solve every problem for nations outside
To put his own house in order he'd be better employed
So get down to work and stop your old jawin'
And give better concessions in Knockadullaun.

We have TDs in West Limerick but what are they doin'
I think like the Russians they're going to the moon
And forgetting poor people in their pitiful plight
When they sit in Dail Eireann they should see things right
And show us some mercy and remove slavery
And give us an hour and a chance of hot tea
Treat us like humans and not amadáns
We're God's creatures too here in Knockadullaun.

A Day in the Bog

The old fashioned manual way of cutting turf with the sleán is quickly disappearing and with the advent of the huge turf-cutting machines the sleán, I'm afraid, will become an item for the museum.

Back through many generations in Ireland the bogs supplied the fuel that heated the homesteads in the rural areas within a reasonable distance where the turf could be transported with horse drawn carts prior to the coming of tractors and lorries. It was the main livelihood of many families living near the bogs, carrying the turf by horse and rail into the towns to supply the demands of the residents for domestic heating, baking, and cooking.

From the bogs of Knocknagorna. Dirreen and Glasha there was an established market in the town of Newcastle West where turf was sold in lots as small as a bag full by regular suppliers. John McMahon, Dirreen carted it all the long way to Rathkeale, starting out in the dark of the winter's morning in hail or rain, sitting on top of the load or in an impoverished seat formed by a wooden board projecting out from the rail on the cart a cold spot on a frosty morning.

In the years before rural electrification the consumption of turf was a great deal more than now, especially with the farming community where big fires were continually burning for cooking, baking and boiling big pots of water to cook the food for hens, ducks, geese and other poultry as well as for calves, cows, pigs and bonhams which were kept in big quantities in every farmyard and it was the custom to serve them with warm food. The water for the cows to drink after giving birth to their calves was warmed up too.

To provide fuel for all this heating, big ricks of turf were needed and many labourers were employed in the cutting, footing, stacking and drawing home of it. Clamping the ricks was undertaken by a man skilled in the job as the rick would be required to stand for twelve months or so for the last of it to be burned and if the clamp was not executed in a professional manner it could come toppling down like the walls of Jericho.

The dimension of the rick would be eleven feet or so broad, rising to a height of seven feet, sloping slightly from the bottom to the top and long enough to contain the required amount of turf. It would be covered on top with rushes to protect it from the falling rain and snow as turf, however dry it would be could not withstand being penetrated and soaked by the rain.

To those accustomed to wield the sleán and fork work didn't seem all that hard but to the beginner it was a very tiring task indeed. It was a constant movement from start to finish without any time to relax and many is the able-bodied man that went home in the evening with painful sides and cramped fingers for no sooner had the man branching after the sleansman a sod removed than there was another one cut in its place. So it was a constant motion which taxed the unpracticed muscle.

Three men were generally engaged in the cutting. One referred to as the sleánsman - cutting it. Another known as the Brancher - forking the turf as it was cut, sod by sod, to a man spreading it out on the sward. The sods would measure four inches square approx. by twelve inches long. The banks generally around this locality were six sods high. The top sod would be cut a shade smaller than the ones beneath it. This brought increased pressure on the man branching for each bench cut made the bank higher and according as the bank was rising, the sods were getting bigger and heavier and easier to cut as the bog was much softer and sods were coming quicker from the sleánsman. So as I've stated already, a man unaccustomed to such work would find it very fatiguing indeed.

To illustrate this I'll tell you of a farmer who hired a man for a few days in the bog. He was a sleánsman himself and I needn't tell you he wasn't too lenient on this man who was branching from him. Not being accustomed to the task the poor man was nearly dead when the day was down. Anyway, as he was leaving the bog to go home the farmer said to him "Don't forget tomorrow". "Well" he replied, "I won't forget today anyway, whatever about tomorrow".

The wheelbarrow was introduced into the production of turf during the war years, first used with Bórd na Móna in the bogs of Offaly where some of our local labourers went to work and they brought back the method to their locality. The wheelbarrow made the task of cutting the turf easier for as heretofore the brancher had to exert his arms a great deal to swing the turf far enough out on the sward so that the man spreading it in neat formation could leave enough space to fit the entire six sods on the portion of the bank remaining between him and the face of the bank.

Now the brancher had merely to lay the turf on the edge of the bank beside him from where the "bank manager" forked it into the wheelbarrow and wheeled it out. No place does the proverb "Practice makes perfect" hold better than in the bog. There I have seen the experienced men working in unison. The sleánsman cutting at a very rapid pace, the brancher laying it neatly on the bank and the man with the wheelbarrow racing in and out so that not a single sod was left lying carelessly around when they reached the end of the plot. It is a delightful sight to see a long bank of turf, neatly spread out on the sward, with the sun beaming on it.

After the turf lying on the sward for three weeks, more or less, depending on the weather, came the backbreaking job of footing it. Like the cutting, this job required practice to enable the worker to make a good hand of it and there was a certain form of making the stook or foot so that the sun and wind could have the advantage of getting at every sod and thus increase the speed of drying it.

In different areas there were different shapes of stooks. Bórd na Móna usually adopted to the method of box-footing. Here in this locality the method employed was placing the sods on end starting with one sod sloping against another then two more sods in the same fashion against those two and one sod horizontally on top of the four. In this way all sods were exposed to the weather.

Footing was not confined to men. In fact, the women were regarded as being more supple to bend their backs to the task as the person footing had to remain continually in a stoop and was often heard groaning with pains in the back and the muscles of the thighs. Yet, like the footballers and others engaged in strenuous sport, practice tones up the muscles and reduces the strain and most people find they can stay stooped all day footing without any complaints of ill effects after the initial start of getting climatised to it.

Back in the years of the Emergency when the Co. Council took over the bogs for turf production to supply fuel for its institutions the women proved their worth in the saving of the nation's fuel when coal was in very short supply. Here in large numbers were women married and single, who were all delighted to get employed, as cash was very scarce in the years preceding World War 11 and many young girls and boys found it hard enough to find the four pence admission into the local dance halls. So it is easy to visualise the eagerness of all to grasp the opportunity that work in the bogs afforded.

The women were not in the fashion of dress then as the girls of today - and more's the pity - for if they were clad in trouser suits instead of long skirts how much more comfortable would they have been, for they were exposed to wind and rain in the bleak mountainside. But they stuck it uncomplaining even that the task at times was extremely hard for the female sex. For instance, the loading of the turf into extra high lorries where the transporters were paid by weight and were anxious to take as much turf as possible to get rich as quickly as possible. This brought extra pressure on those filling the turf which had all to be done by hand. Let it be to the credit of the girls- it was found that six girls loading a lorry could do it in shorter time than the same number of men (six was the usual number filling a lorry) even that the women might be noisier at the job with the odd screech and loud laughter but that only seemed to increase their will and stamina.

Work in the bog was never dull for, in the quietness of the open air (unlike the factory), the conversation was always kept up and the jokes and yarns were spun and romances discussed and dates were made and - the best of all- cash flowed and the lifestyle of the community changed and improved and, in spite of rations, everyone was happy.

CHILDHOOD MEMORIES OF GLIN

The first time I visited Glin was on the occasion of my First Communion in 1926. I was attending Ballguiltenane National School, situated at the southern end of the Glin parish, although I was living in the neighbouring parish of Athea. As I was a pupil of Glin parish school it was reasonable to expect I'd get my First Communion in Glin Parish Church with the rest of my classmates.

The teachers in Ballyguiltenane then were Willie Griffin and his wife who were living in Glin town and came to school in a pony and trap car. Both were very religious and recited the rosary as they came and went on their journey. She was very kind and generous and I remember quite clearly having breakfast in her house on the day of my First Communion as it was law of the church then that those receiving the Eucharist should be fasting from midnight. In her generosity it was her custom to take the boys in Ballyguiltenane into her hospitable home for breakfast on their First Communion day. I'm sure the Lord did reward her, for herself and her husband had a long and happy life together in their comfortable home in Upper Main Street. The houses in Glin appeared awful high to young childhood eyes coming from the country where most of the houses were low thatched dwellings.

Some of those who got their First Communion and sat for breakfast at the table with me on that occasion are gone to share their eternal reward. May they rest in peace.

A few years after, while still a barefoot garsoon, I would occasionally visit my aunt, Johanna Liston, who lived in Church Street, a few houses away from the church.

The road from the square to the Castle gate was lined with large tall trees making it a very picturesque route. Those trees were later cut down and removed and replaced with a smaller variety of tree. One tree opposite the Catholic Church was spared for a long time after the others. It was used for holding posters advertising coming events such as auction of meadowing, elections, dances and concerts. A familiar sight on the route too were the horses, ponies and donkeys with the milk churns on the carts delivering milk to the Dairy Co-op from out-lying farming areas.

Another feature of the town square were the women at the fountain with buckets awaiting their turn to fill up as they chatted and viewed the "going on" around the street. At the time the fountain was the main source of their water supply to many householders. There were wells at a few other locations, one of which is still there today, at the back of John O' Shaughnessy's.

On the square too were horses and donkeys with cartloads of turf for sale transported from the boglands Ballygoughlin, Ballyguiltenane, Dromreask and Scart. A lot of turf was burned then as there were no other means but the fire for heating and cooking. There was, of course, different fuel like coal or timber but the turf seemed to be most satisfactory locally. I remember a poem in my schoolbook which said:

"Woodman spare that tree, touch not single bough,
In my youth it sheltered me, and I'll protect it now".

There was a householder who was short of fuel for the fire and he told the woodman:

"Woodman cut that tree, spare not a single bough,
In my youth 'twas dear to me but turf is dearer now".

Another memory that comes to mind is Glin Pier where I gazed on the provisions of flour, meal, bran, pollard and other foodstuffs being unloaded from boats onto the storehouses on the pier and reloaded onto horsecarts to be transported to the shops in the outlying district, much of it to Athea village.

As I returned from the pier to the town I climbed up the turret tower of the old castle, all that remains is the tower. The castle itself was demolished by Carew and his forces.

Three days we looked forward to during our school days were the two days of Glin Coursing meeting in the first week of October and the day of the old fair as we got those days free from school. Whilst the coursing meeting may be favoured by fine weather the old fair day was generally cold, wet and windy. Those farmers driving cattle into the fair in the early morning had to shiver it out for hours before disposing of them.

On my first visit to the coursing I was fascinated by the broad river Shannon. As I went along from the town to the field I gazed with wonder on the huge size of the Desmond Castle with its many windows to be seen from the coursing field.

To come back again to the town I remember in my early visits seeing the men chatting at the corner or sitting on the window ledges of the shop. Their presence here was so resented by the shop owners that they had steel spikes fitted on the ledges to prevent them using them as a seat.

Conuckeen

To boglands white with canaváns
My thoughts do often stray
From these sunny lands with houses grand
Here in the USA
All the grandeur bright I have in sight
And the dollars that I've seen
Cannot keep my mind from the neighbours kind
I left around Conuckeen

The sweet fresh air that's always there
To bleach the Irish cheek
Cannot be found in this Yankee ground
No matter where you seek
Depressing heat to make you sweat
Not like the Irish green
Where oft' we strode by that bog road
Along by Conuckeen

Where the warbling birds your heart would stir
With songs so gay and bright
And the corncrake the silence break
In the Summers sweet twilight
There the gabhairín ruadh in the evenings dew
In winged flight is seen
Across 'Gragra o'er you will see her soar
At nightfall around Conuckeen

There in days now gone the pike and sleán
We often wielded there
And justice done to a dinner great out in the open air
Oh, what I'd give once more to live
And enjoy the self-same scene
And partake of "tae" in the same old way
From a saucepan in Conuckeen

Many hours we enjoyed on the mountainside
On a Sunday after Mass
There we'd meet with hounds to search around
The countryside across
The big brown hare from the 'gouloughter' there
The turtógs in between
Would twist and turn, with speed to burn
For the greyhounds round Conuckeen

We had many a romance at the old wren dance
With colleens sweet and gay
With their roguery there, a saint from prayer
They would surely coax away
With dance and wine there at O'Briens
Such pleasant sights we've seen
God be with those times in Irish climes
Around you, Conuckeen

Lament for Benjy

Goodbye, goodbye, my dear old friend too soon we had to part
As I lay you beneath the clay there's sadness in my heart
I miss your loving company for you were always there
To welcome me on my return with your kindness rare.

You conveyed me from my doorstep as I on a journey went
And was awaiting my return so full of merriment
You showed me your fond affection in every way you could
You stood guard outside my door as a faithful sentry would.

You were always very wary when you beheld a stranger
And warned me to be on my guard against impending danger
You were the first to look on me as soon as I would wake
And gazed with loving glances as my breakfast I'd partake.

When I asked you to share it shyly you would stand
And ever so gently take it from my proffered hand
Then you'd show your gratitude with a loving smile
From eyes that showed respect and love devoid of guile.

After our good years together I'm now left all alone
Without your presence to cheer me in my coming and my going
As I walk away from your closed grave the tears in my eyes doth
fog
For I miss you, dear old Benjy, my lovely collie dog.

LIFE IN WEST LIMERICK
IN MY FATHER'S TIME

I would like to say something in general about the ways of living here around West Limerick in my father's time. A time when people were generally in poor circumstances and found it difficult to rear their large families. Large families were in vogue and it was a common sight to see families of nine, ten, twelve and more reared in one and two-roomed mud cabins and they all grew up to be tall, strong and healthy. Government aid was non existent, there was no Social Welfare benefit, no Widows and Orphans pensions and no dole.

Looking back I often wonder how the people existed when this country supported eight million people. With very few factories at the time we must gather that the population was supported on the land which must have been worked extensively in spite of the fact that there was none of today's machinery - tractors, rotovators or combine harvesters. They used the horse and plough and, of course, there were more than enough labourers to work the spade and shovel.

Since there was no rural electricity and no milking machines, the dairy farmers had to keep servants continually employed as the cows had to be milked by hand. In those bygone days in the area, where there were more than enough servants to meet the local demands, some attended the hiring fairs in Newcastle West. Here the farmers from East Limerick came to engage the labourers - or servants as they were then called, both boys and girls. The contract was from 1st February until Christmas.

There were many stories told about the hardship that some of those servants endured in the various houses where they worked. Some slept in lofts over stables, with scanty bedclothes and no means of drying their wet clothes or a fire to go near. They were compelled to work long hours for which they received a small remuneration.

Usually the eldest son inherited the farm. The others, where the parents could afford it, were sent to post-primary schools and succeeded in getting white collar jobs. The son inheriting the farm was well-seasoned before the parents handed it over. I suppose they could not very well part with it, seeing as there was nothing for them to survive on until the old age pension came into being. Generally, where the farm was transferred to the son, there was provision made for the parents in the line of keeping a bedroom and being supplied with milk, turf etc.

In other cases the farm was divided between two sons with an addition put to the house to accommodate them or maybe an additional house built. This worked out well in most cases but, on occasion, the older son thought he was done out of his right to inherit the entire farm and it caused bickering and trouble between the brothers, causing much annoyance to both families. A neighbour overheard two brothers in such a position quarreling one day. One said to the other, "You couldn't be good and the mother you had". Apart from incidences such as this, the people of West Limerick were all attached to each other and were ready and eager to help one another at every beck and call. Any family suffering a bereavement could always be sure of help from the neighbours while such help was needed.

The houses at that time were very inferior to the houses of today in rural West Limerick. There is a great improvement made to accommodate our people today and, along every road you travel, magnificent new houses have sprung up with central heating and toilet facilities that our forefathers knew nothing about. However, though they were deprived of carpeted floors and water on tap, they were happy - maybe happier than a lot of the people in their luxurious mansions today. They loved their homes, homes where anyone and everyone could lift the latch and be welcomed with a céad míle fáilte. Homes where you need not discard your boots at the door for you were going to leave no marks on the flagstones as you stepped up to the open fire.

The farmers married their own rank and generally a match was arranged between the parents of the couple or a matchmaker in the district. A fortune (dowry) was demanded by the father of the bridegroom. His farm and means were inspected by the parents of the intended bride before any bargaining for a fortune began. It would appear that means of living was the deciding factor and took priority in all cases. The feelings of the couple towards each other were never considered. In fact, in some cases, the intending couple never met until the whole business was arranged and everything fixed for their wedding.

One fortune might marry what farmers were in one side of a parish. According as a son got a fortune from an incoming bride, he had to hand it over to a sister to get her married to some other farmer and that farmer, in turn, handed it over to his sister and so on until it arrived at someone who had no sister to shift out of the way of the new bride. In the days of arranged marriages it would appear that very few farmers married for love of their partners. If love is necessary to make marriage successful and happy it must have developed later on in their partnership for there weren't many broken marriages then and they all seemed to have lived happily and united ever after.

OUR CELESTIAL GLOBE

Oh! What a great expanse there is between the stars and me,
How they come to be thus placed is man's great mystery,
Nature keeps them in control, in their place they'll stay,
Since time from the beginning rolls as each night follows day.

God is guiding them I'm sure in his heavenly sphere above,
To make our earth and life secure they are wont to move.
In the way that He has willed in that far off sphere,
To make the seasons come and go in light and darkness here.

The moon as well as giving light controls our oceans and seas,
It seems to control our very minds bringing sadness or peace,
What a chaotic state we'd have on this earth here below,
If the moon erroneously behaved
and oceans uncontrolled did go.

If the stars refused to come in view and the sun went on strike,
Confusion would then reign, the God we know would be sought at
night.
Or are we not forgetting Him and taking all for granted here,
Without realising He's the one
that guides our Heavenly sphere.

This world did not come into being just by an accident,
No, all those things and human beings
to earth by God were sent.
Each man on earth was made by God;
each one an entirely separate being,
Different from all others as in our fingerprints can be seen.
Can we believe this was an accident upon our earthly sod,
Even in this age of computers
we can't deny the works of God.

If we behaved in a humane way and like the moon and stars,
Be obedient to our God there would be no awful wars.
No killing of our brothers would shame our country
And we'd be sure of entering our Heavenly home of destiny.

A MURDER COMMITTED

My mind is bent on murder and of God I'm not afraid
For I know he will forgive me when this deed I'll perpetrate
I know my enemy is one of his creatures to fill his place on earth
Considering the evil that he does he should
never have been given birth

He has robbed me of my sleep and disturbed my very brain
I have sworn his life I'll take for he has driven me insane
How can a man his temper hold when he gets no sleep at all
When his privacy is invaded from once the night will fall

When tired and weary I lie down to get much needed rest
I turn off the light switch, then this uninvited guest
Comes pounding oe'r my bedstead like a spirit that is evil
Or a disturbing poltergeist with instructions from the Devil

He dances his merry dance on the floor above my head
I have sworn many a time that I will strike him dead
I have tried in various ways to take his life away
But he's so cunning he evades every scheme I lay

I have asked my God for guidance
I've cursed the invader oe'r and o'er
I have closed tight every window and bolted every door
My daughter fled in terror crying "From this house I'm going"
And I was left to face the music and fight him all alone

I'm not a man to throw in the towel I'm made of tougher mettle
I met the invader face to face and I have won the battle
Once again I can sleep the night there's peace within my house
For I carried my avowed intent and
I murdered that cursed mouse

A Stroll by Newcastle West

As I strolled by the Arra near Newcastle West,
In the lovely twillight ere the sun sank to rest
My mind went wandering to days that are gone,
As I watched the ducks in the river go swimming along.

I sat on the bridge beside the South Quay,
Where the traffic was eager for their right of way,
The motors all speeding as if time was rationed out,
What of the time when the donkey took them about.
They had more time to chat with the neighbours they met.
Now 'tis all hurry and bustle and worry and fret.

My mind went awandering back through the years,
To the ponies and horses who passed o'er the bridge here,
All laden with produce for the Market Yard,
Each week on a Thursday to reap the reward,
Of all their labour, all their endeavour and sweat,
As they sold their goods, they did much pleasure get.

Oats, spuds and turnips and cabbage plants there you'd find.
And scallops for thatching to hold against the wind,
There the squeal of the bonhams, the fat pigs and sows,
The geese and the turkeys were grumbling aloud.

The shouts of the hand-me-down men you would hear.
And their witty tongue to coax customers near,
All kind of clothing for a bargain was going,
In their secondhand stall where many were known.

There on a fair day the town would be full,
With calves, heifers and bullocks, milch cows, an odd bull.
Here jobbers aplenty would be making a deal,
And with their sticks of raddle a bargain would seal.

Then on to the railway the cattle they'd take,
To various destinations more profit to make.

At the heel of the evening with voice loud and clear.
The ballad singers in full tune would appear,
To sing of our patriots who fought, fell and died,
To drive out the foreigners from our countryside.

There in the pubs with throats all well oiled,
They'd talk of the country and the way it was spoiled,
Fists often flew in a heated debate,
When Guinness had put them in a fiery state.

As you'd walk by the shop doors you'd see there displayed.
A sleán or a fork, scythe, shovel or spade,
Or a square of shoe leather, a hammer and last,
And wax, hemp and tacks to mend it on fast.

Rolls of strong hemp there in the harvest time,
To use in the meadows to tie down the wynds,
And an array of saucepans and buckets on show,
Mugs, jugs and kettles, and the enamel po,
Now the scene has all changed the small shops are no more.
All those things are indoors in the big shopping store.

The market yard is now bare of vegetables and all,
'Tis now full of motors who to shopping centres call,
We call it progress as onward they roll,
The sad thing is that progress puts many drawing dole.

A DAY IN THE CARRIGEEN

In the 30's and 40's Limerick County Council was in the act of widening, strengthening and surface dressing the roads to make them capable of taking the heavy traffic which then became the mode of transport that was previously catered for by the railroads.

To obtain material for the job the Co. Council resorted to the stone quarries. Some of those quarries had rather a soft stone which was not very difficult to lift, break or manage, for instance, like the limestone quarries in the eastern end of the County. Quite the contrary here in Blaine near Athea. In this quarry called the Carrigeen the stone was of wild hard flinty nature almost impossible to quarry with crowbars as there were no connecting points as are found in most quarries. Here we had one solid rock. In the circumstances it had to be bored using a compressor and long steel drills. Into the holes was placed sticks of gelignite and detonators which were ignited blasting the rock asunder. Jack O'Connor from Carrickerry was employed in this capacity and he became known as "Jack the Borer". Day after day the compressor was heard pumping the pressure that sent the drills boring and grinding their way down through the hard solid rock sending up the white dust as they sank to ten or twelve feet making a hole 2cm in diameter. The holes were approximately four feet apart. At times the drill got stuck when some loose stone prevented it from spinning. When this happened it took a lot of tugging with a huge spanner to release it. The drills became blunt and ineffective from time to time so to keep them sharpened a skilled man was employed in an open forge with anvil and coal fire and bellows to keep it tuned up for it needed to be very hot to bring the drills to the right temperature when inserted in the red coals.

The temperature was determined by the colour of the drill as it was withdrawn from the fire. The blacksmith then placed it on the anvil and with the assistance of another man with a heavy hammer replaced the sharpened point on the end of the drill. The cutting edge was in the form of a cross and each arm had to be precisely the exact measurement as the others used as it took drills of various lengths to bore the same hole and each one had to follow the other at exactly the same width; so great care had to be taken in the job.

I was assisting Tom Meehan from Knockaderry who was working as a blacksmith in Blaine for a term. In later years they dispensed with the blacksmith when the pattern of the drills was changed and the sharpened end could be replaced with a screwed on chisel. When all the holes were bored in a particular part of the quarry to be blasted some sticks of gelignite were dropped into the holes after removing the cork a fist of grass usually packed on top to prevent any substance falling in that might obstruct the sticks of gelignite from getting to the bottom.

The amount of gelignite placed in each hole depended on its depth and the hardness of the stone to be blasted. On the last stick of gelignite on each hole was inserted a detonator with a length of twin wires attached. When all the holes were fed with gelignite and detonators all the protruding wires were attached to each other, and one wire from the first hole and one wire from the last hole was attached to a lead long enough to be safe from any fallen stones when the blast was set off .

Just before this was about to take place a sentry was placed on each road leading by the quarry to halt and hold up the traffic as well as warning the residents of nearby dwellings. Then Jack the Borer, from his position in Liston's meadow west of the quarry where he had taken up his position at the end of the long lead whistle, pressed the arm on what seemed a square box on the ground that sent the current along the wire. Immediately there was a deafening explosion that sent a black cloud of dust and stones flying in the air out of the bowels of the Carrigeen and around it was the disgusting smell of the gas from the exploded gelignite.

It was after the blast the real hard work started. A group of willing workers was then employed with crowbars, sledgehammers and wheelbarrows as the stones had to be lifted with the crowbars and broken small enough to be fed into the mouth of the stonebreaker whose corrugated jaws would grind them into the required size for road making.

When the stones were quarried, broken and piled in a huge heap after days of backbreaking work, a big black steam engine came along with the stonebreaker and sleeping van attached. The van to accommodate the two men employed in the working of the machinery was parked on a wide margin of the roadside beside the quarry. The first engine driver and his assistant that I remember working in the Carrigeen was Jim Purcell from Kilmallock and Paddy Lynch from Cappamore. Jim seemed old then and not subtle in the limbs.

His life must have been a lonely one for he never went home no matter how long the term of work lasted. Paddy Lynch on the other hand cycled all the way home to Cappamore on his pushbike leaving Blaine after working a half-day on Saturday. It was then a 48 hour working week; that is from 8am till 5.45pm Monday to Friday and from 8am to 12.15pm Saturday. There was just one break for lunch from 12 to 1 o'clock. Paddy was back again on Monday morning to start the fire on the steam engine and have steam up to start breaking at 8am.

Jack Liston was inspired to write a poem about them, which opened with the lines.
"Oh Paddy dear you're welcome here from Cappamore so gay
yourself and Jim those stones to break in Blaine so near Athea.
The Carrigeen that once had been a hill of great renown.
But once they brought their gelignite 'tis quickly tumbling down."
Many of the men with whom I worked at the stone crusher are gone to their well earned eternal reward. May they rest in everlasting peace from the noise and dust in Blaine. Some of the locals who have died are Jack (Marshall) Mc Mahon a great man with crowbar or sledge-

hammer. Dick Enright who was never caught idling, two Histon brothers Jack and Bill and Donie Shine, Thade Ahern, Joe Vaughan, Flahertys Jack and Paddy, Tom Lynch, Paddy Langan, Paddy (Boyo)Shine, Ned Grady, Paddy Fitz, Jim Connors, Jack Carroll, Padden and Bill Mulvihill and the impartial and common sense ganger Mike Scanlan lower Dirreen who never slept it out.

There was nothing about the art of the quarrying or breaking stones that Mike did not know. For instance a strong man could be wielding a sledge with all his might without any effect but let Mike come along, place the stone in a different position and with less force with the hammer the stone fell apart. Just as a tree grows with a grain in it. It's like a knot on a tree that makes it almost impossible to split it so also you'll find a similar knot on a stone that you could not get to yield to the hammer. Here again Mike Scanlan showed his knowledge and would come to the relief of the man who was tiring himself trying to get the better of it.

Mike would silently wave him away and then dump unyielding rock where it would never be found. The crusher was placed in position by the side of the clamped heap of stones. A long board belt travelling from a big wheel on the steam engine to a smaller belt on the crusher kept revolving to keep the jaws grinding against each other with great force that sent the broken gravel rolling down in great quantities through revolving round steel screen that separated it into different components. The bigger gravel travelled through the screen and tumbled out at the end, the smaller stones went through the holes and came out in a separate pile. The chips came through another apartment and the dust fell down at the entrance to the screen.

All this material had to be removed with a shovel as it came spilling out. That might look to you a very ordinary job but ask anyone who spent a day at the breaker in Blaine or elsewhere and he'll tell you what a tiring and painful task it was. So many cubic yards of broken material was demanded daily by the engineers and to obtain the required amount the crusher couldn't be left idling for one minute of the day.

Seven men were usually employed directly with the crusher, one man feeding the stones, two men throwing the stones up to him on the platform, one man removing the dust and finished chips with a wheelbarrow, one man shovelling away from the side of the screen, and two men at the end of the screen where the spills tumbled out in never ceasing abundant quantities.

The arms of those men shovelling were taxed to the very limit often to the point of despair as the towering mound of gravel onto which they were shovelling was growing higher and higher and they had to endeavour to pitch stones over the top of this to keep it from encroaching on their limited workspace. The job was so strenuous that the workers had to have a change of jobs every two hours. The proverb "a change is as good as a rest" proved very true here. Increasing the agony of the workers was the unbearable cruelty of the dust swirling from the breaker and settling on the head, faces and eyes. Everyone looked as if he were wearing a mask, all you could see was his two tormented eyes appearing through the white dust cemented with sweat on his face. The dust also entered his mouth and nostrils and down his throat and thick spittles of dust were discharged from his choked throttle and larynx.

ECCLESIASTICAL BLUNDERS

In a parish one time it happened that the parishioners got awful careless about their religious duties and in the finish there were only very few going to Mass. The priest decided to bring on the Missioners for a week hoping that the holy Fathers, as we called them, would change the situation and bring back the people to the church and the Sacraments. On the opening night of the mission the priest was surprised to see only one person in the church. He didn't know what to do. He went to the man who was sitting in the front seat to talk to him about the situation. "Well Father", said the man, "if I went out to feed the hens and if only one hen turned up I'd feed that one." "I suppose you have a point there" said the priest, so he went back on the Altar and started off the Rosary then a Sermon and Benediction, which was the usual programme at the time. He went to talk to the man again and asked him what he thought of the situation. "The way I look at it," said the man, "if I went out to feed the hens and if only one hen turned up, I wouldn't throw her the whole bucket of mess."

Well after a few nights the Congregation came back and in answer to the Priest's pleading they went to Confession but had been so careless about their religion that they had forgotten what Sin was. Anyway the man went to Confession, the priest asked him "Well my child, what's troubling you?" "Well Father" said he "I have a big sin and a small sin to confess." "Very well " said the priest " we'll take the small sin first, what is it?" " I shot a Tan Father", said he. "What was the big sin you committed?" said the priest, " I missed the other two Father".

During the mission there was a couple getting married and after they were wed they went into the Sacristy to sign the Marriage Register. The man was very low-sized and the woman was extra tall. The priest being in good humour said to the man "Hadn't you great courage to take on such a tall woman", "yerra" said the man "what extra charge would I want. Anyone would swear the way you're talking that shes going to be always standing."

Another one of the missioners was a long bearded Priest and as he was preaching, a woman in the front seat was sad and weeping an odd tear. The priest approached her after the ceremony being over and asked her what she found so touching in his Sermon that caused her to weep. "Well Father" she said, "as I was looking at you with your chin and your whiskers bobbing up and down you reminded of my little goat that died last week."

The priest then decided to make a call on the old people around the Parish. He went into this house where the woman had a pot of soup ready for her dinner and being a hospitable sort of person she invited the priest to partake in some. The priest didn't like to refuse her for fear she'd be offended so he accepted her offer and she filled him out a bowl of soup. As he was drinking it a pet bonham that was in a tea chest box in the corner ran out squeaking, and looking up at him "Isn't he a very cute little Bonham" said the priest "wouldn't you think it's how he knows me?" "It isn't you he knows at all Father" said the woman "but he knows his own little bowleen".

A Parish Priest employed a maid who was very industrious and satisfactory in every way. The only thing the Priest didn't relish was when she'd be talking of different items she'd say *your* chairs *your* this and that and so on. "Mary" he said to her one day, "wouldn't it be more homely to both of us if you used the word "our" instead of "your" when you are referring to things in the house." Mary agreed to do that and all was going fine until the Bishop came to the Parish administering the Sacrament of Confirmation. When the ceremonies were over, the Parish Priest and the Bishop and other Priests from the neighbouring parishes were sitting down to tea. Mary burst into the room screaming as if she was being murdered, "What's the matter Mary" asked the Parish Priest, "Oh good God Father" said she "there's a big mouse under *our* bed".

The Missioners

"My mind it often wanders back to memories of the past,
When times were far more leisurely and life was not so fast,
No radio or telly to disturb our sweet content,
And the coming of the Missioners was a much discussed event."

How well do I remember the Missioners coming to preach and bless
the parish and the people of Athea when Fr. Rea was parish priest
there. It was in the 1920's. I was then living in Glasha in one of the
last houses in the north-eastern end of the parish. Higgins was my
nearest neighbour - in fact it was the last house four miles or so from
the church.

Canon Rea as he later became, did much towards the improvement of
the church in Athea, bringing comfort to the congregation attending
services there. Before he was appointed parish priest in Athea I
remember the seating was very scarce - I remember when there were
only a dozen seats in the main aisle. What a difference from kneeling
on the bare tiles to the padded kneelers we have today. It was also
during Fr. Rea's time in Athea that the church walls were wainscoted
and seats provided for the entire church.

As well as being concerned with the bodily comforts of his people he
was also very enthusiastic about the state of their souls and arranged
a sodality and apportioned the parish in different sections, with two or
three townlands in each section, and each section was placed under
the patronage of a saint. I remember the townlands of Upper and
Lower Dirreen and my townland of Glasha were under the patronage
of St. Patrick. The idea of this was that, when the people went to
communion every month as they were obliged to do, the name of the
saints representing their group would be displayed on a high staff held
by rings fastened to the end of a seat and your group had to occupy
the seats immediately behind your particular saint. This was to make
it easy for the appointed steward in each group to note whether you

were present or absent from your monthly sodality as a check was being kept. Pat Shine of Dirreen was the man in charge of the group of which I was a member.

There was a separate Sunday in the month for the women's sodality. Any member found to neglect his duties when the roll book would be inspected by the P.P. would be reminded of it and requested to keep up the good practice. So great was the reverence for the priest and so great was the love and fear of God then that only very few would refuse to accede to any request or demand the Canon would make.

During Canon Rea's time in Athea there was a Guard Rowsome stationed in the Garda Barracks. There was also in Athea a man by the name of Ruck Drury of a poetic mind. One day the Canon remarked to him on the unusual name of Drury as there was no other one of the name in the parish. "Well, Father", said Drury, "Ruck Drury, Rowsome and Rea are the three rarest names in the parish of Athea". As I'm at it, I may as well tell you about the Canon accusing old Tom Langan of Glasha of leaving the church just before the Mass had finished. Tom was very old then, after serving a lot of his life in the British Army out around Egypt and the Holy Land. "Why are you leaving the church before the blessing or do you believe in Jesus Christ?" the Canon asked. "Why not?", said Tom, "wasn't I outside where he was born".

Tom was a very courageous and fearless man. One winter's night he was in Athea with his donkey and cart. It was pouring rain and Rice Danaher had compassion for him. "Tom, how are you going to get home to Glasha on a night like this?". "How did I get home from Baghdad?", said Tom.

Another thought that strikes me is the procession on Corpus Christi through the village, where every house would be painted and holy pictures and flowers displayed to honour the divine presence of Our Lord passing by. The procession generally proceeded down the street from the church, swung around near the bridge and back up again to the top of the town. The Rosary would be recited on the way and Benediction would finish the ceremony in the open at the top of the street. On a few occasions I remember Canon Rea engaging St. Joseph's Brass Band from the Industrial School in Glin, run by the Christian Brothers. The band marched at the head of the procession down the street and turned at Batt's corner up the Abbeyfeale Road for a short distance and entered a field of Wrenn's on the right where devotions were held before returning to march back to the town. What a glorious sight to behold - to see the great crowd assembled together as the sun shone down and the gentle breeze blew across the fragrant hillside. Our thoughts went back to the Penal days when Mass was celebrated in the open in secret places to escape the enemy when foreign laws prohibited the Mass from being offered.

Once every five years the Missioners, usually two from the Redemptorist Order came to Athea parish for two weeks. There were no amplifiers then for they didn't need them - their loud voices would echo off the walls as they drove the fear of God into the huge congregation that regularly attended. Athea parish must have been very thickly populated at the time that I'm referring to as every night the church was packed and a crowd also attended the morning devotions at 7.00 a.m. - the most of them on shanks mare! It was a common sight to see the road thronged with pedestrians and you must remember that there were three large galleries in the church then, almost doubling the space of today. Yet, in spite of all that, I've seen some of the younger folk placed inside the altar rails for want of space.

To set off the expenses of bringing the Missioners, tickets were issued and a little charge demanded for the seating in the church. The seats in the long aisle, being more comfortable, were threepence for a seat and the others in the short aisles and galleries were twopence, if I remember rightly.

On the kitchen walls of every home in the parish there hung holy pictures and the Sacred Heart lamp. Holy pictures also hung on the walls of the bedrooms where children slept. Now the children have the walls decorated with pictures of pop stars. Anyway, on the street beside the chapel gate during the Mission, the traders pitched their stalls, selling statues, holy pictures, scapulars, rosary beads and holy water fonts and many other pious objects which would be blessed towards the end of the Mission.

Usually one of the two Missioners who came would be a young jolly fellow who told jokes intermingled in his sermons whilst the other would be an older commanding figure who wouldn't take any nonsense and of whom the congregation stood in awe. There used to be a great congregation on the night the humorous man would be preaching, and more penitents around his confessional.

My father, who was born 133 years ago, used tell of an incident that took place outside the confessional where a long queue was waiting to enter. A woman, telling her sins in a loud voice, confessed that she stole a pot. Later on, there was confusion as some of those waiting were trying to get in front of others. The priest came out of the box to restore order and said to one man, "How long are you here?". "I'm here since the woman stole the pot", he said!!

One night, as the Missioner was preaching on the bible, he talked of the woman of ninety who, by a miracle from God, gave birth to a child, having no children before that. A humorous man from Knockanare whom I sat beside nudged me and whispered: "If she was living in Knockanare she wouldn't go to ninety without having a child".

However, to return to the Missioners. When appealing to sinful people to reform their ways I remember the words I so often heard them shout - "Just make a new beginning for it never is too late". Another expression from their sermons I will quote which still echoes in my ears - "What does it profit a man to gain the whole world and lose his one immortal soul".

Working on Sunday was a crime against God and the preachers condemned it with great vehemence. But nothing made the people more attentive than when they talked on the sixth commandment. There were many red faces amongst the courting couples who were the greatest offenders in the priest's eyes and laws of the church at that time. Here again I will quote from their appealing cry - "Beware of those lonely places, keeping company till late at night. He that loves the danger shall perish therein".

The Missioners brought the grace of God to the parish and all the hard drinkers took the pledge and everyone vowed to sin no more. Then, on the closing night, the Missioners were full of praise for all the people and expressed their gratitude for the way they attended the Mission and then came the final prayers, renouncing the devil under a blaze of candlelight. When the priest, on one of these occasions, asked "Do you renounce the devil" one over zealous man was heard to say in a very loud voice "I do, the h**r".!!

Storytelling

Radio, television and videos have changed the face of rural Ireland and wiped out many of our old customs and ways of entertainment. Gone are the days when the neighbours gathered around the fireside at night to play music or dance or sing "Come all ye's" as they were called from the fact that many ballads started off with the words "Come all ye lads and lasses", "Come are ye loyal heroes", "Come all ye true brave Irishmen" etc.

Gone too, and more's the pity, is the art of storytelling and all the pleasure and thrills attached to it for young and old. Stories of giants, leprechauns, witches, fairies, magicians, ghosts etc. used to make people afraid to go home alone in the dark.

Back two generations or more ago there dwelt a man by the name of Tom Connors about a mile east of Blaine Cross on the Kerryline, a grandfather of Mrs. Mary Dalton, Glasha. Here in his comfortable abode the neighbours gathered and listened to him relate in rare fashion or read aloud stories of every kind and colour. My father was one of those who attended those sessions. He must have great brains for remembering for he was able to relate, in minute detail, every story he heard to us his children many years after and 'twas us got the crack from listening as we climbed upon his knees.

I'd like to say in passing that the above-mentioned Tom Connors kept a diary over the years of all local and historical events, births, deaths and marriages, prices at fairs and so on. His grandaughter Moll told me that Thomas (Launy) Culhane, the noted scholar and historian from Ballyguiltenane came to her house in search of the said diaries and was extremely disappointed to learn that Tom's son, Mick, had destroyed them in his old age not realising the harm he was doing. Thomas claimed they would be of immense interest and value to him.

Now to return to my storytelling, I am sorry to say I have most of my father's stories forgotten (shame on me) and they were many. Some of them I have heard by seannachais since - including famous Eamonn Kelly. Others I have never heard or read since my father related them so I am going to make an effort now to recall one of them and I am wondering if any of you readers have heard it I will try and tell it as 'twas told to me.

BILLY AND THE BULL

Once upon a time there lived this man who was very well to do. He owned a big farm with fifty cows and a bull. He had a big mansion of a house, a paved yard with a flagged footpath all around the house, outoffices for the cows and stables for four horses, two for working on the farm and two for the saddle. One he rode himself, the other was for his wife whom he lately married. She rode sidesaddle on her horse beside him for they usually rode out together. She was very beautiful and very generous to the poor who often came to her house looking for alms.

As time went by a baby boy was born to them whom they christened Billy. That was the baby that got attention! I needn't tell you, they were delighted. As the child grew up it was plain to be seen that he was developing the good looks of his mother.

Their joy was brought to an abrupt ending. One day whilst they were riding along a greyhound darted out a gap in hot pursuit of a hare. Her horse bolted and she was thrown from the saddle on to the roadway receiving injuries from which she shortly after died.

The poor husband was heartbroken after the loss of such a beautiful and loving wife and it made him sadder still to think of their only son left motherless. Even that they had a maid employed who did all she could to care for the boy, she could not give him the affection and love of his mother which is so essential towards any child in the development of their good nature and good qualities.

91

Some years passed but the father's grief continued. One day a friend of his advised him that it would be both in his own interest and in the best interests of his son if he considered getting married a second time. At first he would not listen for it was the last thought in his head to bring in a stepmother. He loved his wife so much that he thought he'd be unfaithful to her to place her son in the care of a stepmother.

But, as time went by and after a great deal of advice and persuasion from his friend, he gave in. Moreover when his friend assured him that he had a partner for him that would be as loving, as kind and gentle as his late wife. "Anyway," said he, "who could be otherwise to such a charming little boy as your son Billy"?

The match was made. He married again and all went well. Other children were born from the second marriage but, after a time, the stepmother got jealous of Billy - he was so much better looking than her own children and her mind filled with the thought that his father was showing more love and affection for him than he was towards the children of the second marriage.

Billy, at this time, was in his teens and his stepmother treated him cruelly, hiding the fact from her husband. She sent him out each day herding the cows. He had to drive them to pasture each morning, stay with them during the day until he'd drive them home for milking each night. She would not allow him take any food and gave him very little when he came home, hoping in this way that he'd fall ill and die. He was so frightened of her that he did not complain to his father.

But, much to her surprise, she noticed as the weeks went on that Billy was growing fatter and taller day by day. To solve this mystery she sent her daughter to spy on him. His stepsister stole after him one day and hid where she could not be seen but, at the same time, had a clear view of Billy and the cattle.

Imagine her surprise when at midday the bull came and lay down beside Billy. She watched in amazement as she saw him unscrew the horn from the bull's head, take from it a cloth which he laid on the ground. Soon there appeared on the cloth all kinds of eatables meat, eggs, bread, potatoes and everything and anything you could wish for. When Billy had satisfied himself, what he had left over disappeared as quickly as it had come so he replaced the cloth in the horn and screwed it back on the bull's head.

His stepsister ran home to her mother and poured out her story. The mother changed colours with rage and jealousy but then a wry smile crept over her wicked face. Her mind was forming a plan to get rid of the bull. She arranged for the butcher to come prepared to kill the bull three days later.

On that day, after Billy had partaken of his dinner as usual and replaced the bull's horn, the bull spoke to him and said, "Billy, tonight when you drive the cows and myself home I will be last in line. When the cows have passed into the yard jump on my back. Don't hesitate for a moment as my life is in danger".

That evening all was in readiness for the slaughter of the bull. The butcher was there with hatchet and knife, the workmen with ropes ready to tie him down. To their amazement they saw Billy jump on the bull's back and off they went like a shot off a gun. Although the butcher travelled after them on horseback he had to return without catching a glimpse of the departing bull. The bull and Billy kept going for miles and miles and miles.

It was midsummer, a grand bright mild night. In the finish the bull came to this lovely green valley where he stopped and told Billy to dismount. Billy did. Then the bull told him to take the cloth from his horn and satisfy his appetite. The bull rested while Billy was eating. "Find a cosy spot now", said the bull, "and have a sleep. I am about to be challenged here by another bull whom I'll have to fight but don't you be worried for I'm confident that I can beat him".

Billy lay down and was so tired after his exciting journey that he was soon asleep. He wasn't long asleep, however, when he was awakened by the roaring of a huge bull approaching. He shivered with fright as he saw both bulls engage in what must have been the most ferocious battle ever seen. The bellowing could be heard all over the valley for miles and the ground shook around him with the prancing and plunging. Billy's heart was sinking as he saw his bull being driven backwards but, in one last desperate effort, he plunged forwards and gored the other bull to death.

He then lay down beside Billy to keep him warm for the night. Next morning they started off again over hill and dale, stopping only to eat. Billy was enjoying the trip, viewing the beautiful scenery as he sped along sitting comfortably on the bull's back as relaxed as if he was sitting in a carriage or a motor car. Of course, there were no motor cars then - in fact, there were very few roads. But roads didn't matter to this bull for he could leap over walls, hedges, rivers and rocks. Over mountains and valleys they went until the night fell and again they stopped to rest. The bull had the same story as the night before - another battle with a bull even bigger than the one he killed the night before. He succeeded in killing this one as well.

Anyway, on the third night of their journey the same fate awaited them - another battle! This time the bull said to Billy "I'm afraid this might be my last fight No bull has ever got the better of this bull but there is no way of avoiding this fight" Billy's stomach felt sick on hearing this and the tears came to his eyes for he was now in a strange land all alone. The bull, seeing Billy so lonesome looking, tried to cheer him up saying "Even that I am killed there's a bright future before you . When you'll see me dead cut a length of skin from my side, it will form a belt around your waist. Then take a rib from my side, it will turn into a cane. Anything you'll catch whilst wearing this belt, no matter how heavy it is, you can easily raise and anything you'll strike with the cane will fall before you". It was hard to console Billy for he was heartbroken to think himself and the bull were to be parted.

At that moment he could hear in the distance the bellowing of the approaching bull so he hid with fear and trembling behind a clump of trees. I won't go in here to all the story in detail of this fight as my father used to tell it in such exciting and dramatic fashion which thrilled us in our childhood days. I'll just tell you that Billy's bull was killed. After the other bull left the scene Billy came out of his hiding place. With a heavy heart he cut the magic belt and the magic cane from the bull and set off alone on his lonely and lonesome trail in this unknown country.

As night was falling he saw this big farmhouse. He went in to seek rest for the night or with the chance of getting employment. The boss, who was an extensive farmer, asked him what work he was skilled in doing. "Herding cattle", replied Billy. 'Very well", said the boss, "you're just the man I want. Come in, you can start work in the morning".

Billy drove the cows to pasture as he had done at home and back to be milked at night. One day as he was herding he was roaming around. He came to this very high stone wall. Curious to see what lay beyond it he struck the wall with his magic cane. Immediately the wall came tumbling down, opening up a big gap. Billy went through the gap and there saw a big castle surrounded by large fields of ver- dant green grass. He said to himself that it was a pity to see all this grass going to waste so he drove the cows into the fields to feast on the appetizing grass.

Then he heard the roaring and looking up saw a big giant coming towards him. The giant demanded an explanation from Billy for his conduct. An awful quarrel developed. The end of it was that he offered the giant to fight a duel. The giant laughed at the thoughts of the midget of a man challenging such a huge giant as himself but he said to Billy, "Well, little man, which way do you want to fight. A swing by the back, a battle with a sword or a square round of boxing ?" "A swing by the back", said Billy as he tightened his belt.

The giant approached Billy with one hand extended to catch him, as he thought, and squeeze him to death. But before he realized what was happening Billy had him by the waist and, with one almighty jump, he arose sixty feet in the air with him and threw him with such force that he sunk to his waist in the ground. Billy reached for the giant's sword and was about to cut off his head. The giant pleaded, "Save my life", the giant said, "and I'll give you the keys to my castle, my lands and my property. I'll leave this very day and never return to this country again".

Billy's heart was full of compassion for he was affectionate and gentle like his mother so he lifted the giant out of the ground. The giant signed over all his property and departed on the spot glad that he was taking his life with him.

Billy opened the castle door with the keys and his eyes spread in his head when he saw the luxury of furniture, suites, sofas, beds and carpets etc. There was a large bed for the giant himself but Billy soon disposed of that. In the stables in the yard were beautiful horses, shining harness and carriages.

Billy pretended nothing. He drove the cows home as usual but, when his day's work was done, he stole back again to his castle, changed his attire and drove out on horseback or in one of the carriages. The people wondered who was this nobleman in the lap of luxury but no one knew.

It so happened that the sea was surrounding this part of the country and once in every fifty years, on May Day, a huge monster came in to claim the daughter of the King ruling at the time. If the monster's request was not acceded to he would come out of the water and kill everyone in the district. The King at this particular time had the most beautiful daughter one could ever lay eyes on, just gone nineteen years of age. It brought great sorrow on her parents and on the whole country to know that such a beautiful girl should be sacrificed in this fashion.

Billy heard of the fate that awaited the girl. When May Day came a huge crowd assembled to witness the awful catastrophy about to be enacted. The monster was there, frightening in its size. If the tallest man stood on his lower jaw his head wouldn't reach his upper jaw. There was a hush among the crowd when a nobleman of fine physical proportions rode up on an elegant steed. He quickly dismounted, handed the bridle to one of them to hold, and made his way towards the King and his daughter. The King at this time was almost in the act of throwing his daughter to the monster.

Billy waved the crowd back and stood between the monster and the King. Then he spoke to the monster: "If you mean to take the King's daughter, you won't take her without having to fight for her". The crowd gazed in awe, fearful for their own lives and wondered what revenge the monster would wreak. The monster seemed to understand Billy's statement for he gave a lurch that sent a wave of water over the entire crowd that almost swept them into the sea. With another jump he rose completely out of the water and was ready to descend on the land but Billy rose too and, with one stroke of his magic cane, he severed the head of the monster completely off. The body fell lifeless back into the sea, painting it red with blood. Billy took the head and threw that too back into the water where it sank and that ended the reign of the terrible monster.

Billy had difficulty in getting back to his horse for everyone in the crowd wanted to embrace him, no one more so than the King and his daughter who managed to cut a lock of hair from his curly head. When Billy got away he rode back to his castle, stabled his steed, changed his attire and drove home the cows as if nothing unusual had happened and no one associated him with the drama of the King's daughter.

The King was determined, however, to find his daughters rescuer. He arranged a big party at his castle where everyone within a large radius around were compelled to attend. Billy was there in his ordinary attire but the King's daughter was prepared to scrutinise every guest paraded before her and, noticing Billy's golden locks, invited him to dance with her so that she could view him more closely. She didn't fail to notice the missing locks which she cut and had in her possession. "You are the man that killed the monster", she said. "Indeed I'm not", he replied. Then she produced the lock of his hair and, of course, it matched perfectly.

Billy was forced to admit so he asked leave to be excused for a while and he would return again. He went back to his castle, changed into his rich robes, saddled his horse and rode back to the King's castle where he left no doubt in their minds that he was the man that killed the monster.

Soon after, there was another ball at the King's castle - this time to celebrate the wedding of Billy and the King's daughter and they lived happily together ever after.

My Return
to Coole West

Long years ago I left my home to cross the ocean wide
I bade farewell to all my friends along by the Galeside
Since then in countries far away by good times I was blessed
But I ne'er forgot my own dear spot in lovely sweet Coole West

Each day that's gone brought memories
back of good times long ago
With the comrades of my youth when rambling we did go
All the joys of my young life come throbbing in my breast
And I heave a sigh for the days gone by
In lovely sweet Coole West

No one can tell the grief that haunts a lonely exile's mind
As he dreams of home and those he loved
in the place he left behind
The thoughts of home invades his heart
and the land St. Patrick blessed
There the sweet fresh air that all can share
in lovely sweet Coole West

Well I remember the great crack with
companions light and gay
Many is the happy hour we spent in the dancehall in Athea
Going home by the roadside our Colleens we caressed
As the moon shone bright on a summers night
o'er lovely sweet Coole West

Sometimes in fancy I fondly gaze on Coole West green hillside
What a gorgeous scene there to behold of the country far and wide
Most of Munster can be seen from off its hallowed crest
Oh what I'd give once more to live in lovely sweet Coole West

Thank God my wish is granted lady luck did smile on me
Now I have returned from my exile o'er the sea
My heart with joy is throbbing and my body is refreshed
Each night and day to God I pray for my return to Coole West

Once more I gaze across the vale
on the green fields of Templeathea
And on that holy graveyard where my fore fathers lay
To be laid beside them when I die is my last fond request
Within easy view of home I knew in lovely sweet Coole West

Tribute to Ireland
1962

Ireland, saintly Ireland thou pearl of emerald green
No jewel is there to equal you by any King or Queen
You're a gem from God's own Holy Crown
Where his grace forever flows
To sanctify your children and keep His faith aglow

The cruel hand of the oppressor for years did try in vain
The Holy Faith in Ireland from its people loyal to drain
Its now over 1500 years since St Patrick blessed our clover
And the fire of faith that he lit then is still
burning bright as ever

To every place throughout the globe your holy men have gone
To teach and preach the faith of God
as was ordained by His Son
And with His grace they all succeed
against such dreadful odds
And they triumph like St. Patrick to banish pagan gods

Your gems shine out through learned sons
Who hold high rank and stations
To lead the people here at home and abroad in other nations
The descendants of your Irish too are gleaming on their way
Like John Fitzgerald Kennedy President of USA

Lime-Kilns

Long ago a lime-kiln was built in every farm as burned lime was used extensively in the fertilising of land locally. The lime-kiln was built with stones in the shape of a cone of various sizes. Generally, they were built into the side of a hill so that the top would be level with the land overhead for feeding the kiln and level at the bottom for the removal of the burned lime. Most of those kilns have been demolished now.

The limestones were transported by horse and cart from a place called Cregarde near Shanagolden. It was then broken into small particles with napping hammers. The kiln was filled by first placing a layer of turf at the bottom of the kiln (small turf or black ciaráns were the best for this job). Next a layer of limestones, then another layer of turf and so on until the kiln was filled to the top. Then the turf at the bottom was set afire and according as the limestones burned they fell to the bottom and were shovelled through the eye of the kiln (the eye was an opening at the front at ground level, expertly built so that the lime could be removed easily). Then another "brat" was added to the top of the kiln as it lowered from the top according as it was taken at the bottom. Once the kiln was set to fire, it had to be kept burning day and night until the required amount of lime was burned.

Sowing Potatoes

Whilst each farm was small yet in the bygone time sufficient corn, cereals and vegetables were grown to fulfil the needs of the people, apart from the growing of wheat, oats, barley, turnips, mangolds, cabbage, and of course potatoes which formed the main diet were home produced.

The potatoes were sown mainly in "bawn ridges". These ridges were formed by firstly laying a line - usually the length of the field in which the potatoes were to be planted. The ground was cut with a spade along this line which was then laid four feet or so away from the cut, parallel with it and another cutting made and so on. Between these cuts, about one foot from the edges, was placed a continuous spread of farmyard manure or cowdung as we called it. On top of this was placed the "skillauns" or seed potatoes, about ten inches apart just inside the edge of the manure, a row on each side. Now a "taibhóid", which was a thin sod turned in on top of each row of potatoes, was turned with the spade. When this was done another row of seed potatoes was placed along the centre covered with a sod taken from the furrow. When the garden was finished it consisted of long ridges about two feet wide each containing three rows of potatoes.

Mothers' Legacy

There are many things that I have lost
On my journey on through life
When on its waves I have been tossed
Among the stress and strife.
There is one thing more dear than gold
I've guarded zealously
The little prayers that I was told
upon my mother's knee.

There, with her kind and gentle voice
I can feel her presence still
As she held me clasped upon her lap
My childish mind to fill
And sow the seeds of God's own Grace
To reap eternity
And hand me down the little prayers
She learned on mother's knee

My mind is sometimes full of care
In this world of sorrow and plight
And often now with weary limbs
I do retire at night
But ere my eyes doth close in sleep
No night will escape me
Without I whispering the prayers
I learned on mother's knee

Then in the morning as I awake
To salute another day
Before my head the pillow leaves
Those little prayers I say
The joys and crosses of the day
To offer up to Thee
In the simple words that I was taught
Upon my mother's name

Now from a child I have grown up
And a father I've become
I return thanks to God above
For his blessings on my home
His little gifts of children
He has sent down to me
To carry on the little prayers
I learnt on mother's knee

Moonlight in Glenbawn

Sean: How sweet it was to ramble as old sweethearts long ago

and: When the sun had gone to rest and the twinkling stars

Peg: did glow

With the dewdrops softly falling along the verdant lawn

And with love our hearts were bulging when 'twas

moonlight in Glenbawn.

Seán: As I looked into your eyes so radiant and gay

My heart was so enraptured that my cares all flew away

I was so full of life and vigour I could plough the rocks

of bawn.

Looking forward to the fun I'd have when 'twas

moonlight in Glenbawn.

Peg: Then you told me how you loved me as you shyly stole a

kiss.

You promised to be faithful and fill my life with

bliss.

Sean: And I said Peg darling will you marry me and I'll toil for

you from dawn.

Peg: Sure I could not then refuse you when 'twas moonlight in

Glenbawn.

Sean: Then I took you to the church to wed to make you my

sweet bride.

Peg: With the best man and the bridesmaid as a witness by our side

Sean: There I married you my darling Peg

Sean: And I took you dear Sean

Sean: And we thought we were in heaven when

& Peg 'twas moonlight in Glenbawn.

Sean: I thought I was in Heaven 'til you woke me up one cold wintry night

When I heard your loud complaining you put me in a fright

With my trousers stuck on back to front and my senses nearly gone

I had to run off for the midwife when 'twas moonlight in Glenbawn

Peg: We have nine children now around us praying to God that they'll survive

You stagger home from work each evening looking more dead than alive

You keep snoring like a tractor from nightfall until dawn

Sean: Faith, I think the fun is over when it's moonlight in Glenbawn.

Nativity Play

Joseph
"The road is long dear Mary get ready we must go
To sign our names in Bethlehem though
it looks like frost and snow
Oh God protect us on our way and guide us safely there
We place ourselves all in your hands and in your loving care"

Mary
"I'm ready now dear Joseph all things I've carefully packed
For that long and weary journey across the rugged tracks
So off we go now Joseph and keep a cheerful mind
Although the snow is falling and bitter is the wind."

Joseph
"Thank God at last we have arrived
but look how the crowds appear
I'm worried for your sake Mary lest we get no lodging here
Kind Sir would you have room tonight
for two who have travelled far
All the way from Nazareth cold and hungry now we are."

Inn-keeper
"Begone you little beggar begone now from my door
My house is full of gentry. I have no room for the poor."

Joseph
"No room for us there, Mary. Keep up your heart Asthore
Here we have another inn I'll knock upon the door
Maybe kind Sir you'd have room
to spare for the two of us tonight?"

Inn-keeper
"No room whatever so get away in a hurry from my sight!"

Joseph
"Look yonder through the window look at the beckoning light
I'll enquire maybe we'd have some luck and
there get room tonight"
I beg you kind sir to give us room all inns we've tried in vain
But you appear a kindly man you might
shelter us from the rain"

Inn-keeper
"I'm very sorry I have no room for you and your sweet bride
And I fear that every house is packed
and you will not get inside
But in a stable of mine across the way there is an ass and ox
And you can share it with them - 'tis built in yonder rocks.
I do not mean to offend in offering this to you
For indeed you have my sympathy
and this is the best that I can do."

Joseph
"Thank you very kindly sir. Come Mary let us get there
And take the shelter of the cave in from this freezing air."

Mary
"Joseph go to the store and find for us a meal
And leave me here to rest and pray for very tired I feel."

Narrator
And soon the cave with heavenly light was suddenly aflame
And in a moment of delight the baby Jesus came
Then to the shepherds on the hill the angels came with joy
To tell them that the Saviour was born in Bethlehem nearby.

Angels

"We have come with glad news that the Saviour is born.
Go to him and adore
He is the Christ child who is going to be King
as God promised you before."

Shepherds

"What shall we take as a gift to the child
who came to this world tonight?"
"We take three lambs the best in our flock –
they're so gentle and full of delight."
"Hosanna to the first Noel. Born is the King of Israel."

Narrator

The mind of three wise men in the
East a gleaming star inspired
'Til they read its holy message in the way that God desired
Quite eager then to see and adore the nanmade son of God
Prepared themselves for the long long road
and on their way they trod.

Wise Men

"Look at the star. 'Tis leading us. Let us follow it along
We're prepared for the road and our camels are so strong
When we will find Him these gifts we'll unfold
Frankincense and myrrh and pure shining gold.
Look the star is descending it has come to a stop
I think our journey is ended we can lay aside our map
I can see the heavenly radiance coming through the door
Let us take our gifts and enter, kneel down and adore."

MY OLD MOUNTAIN HOME

Won 1st place in Fleadh Ceoil Limerick newly composed ballads in 2002

My fancy oft takes me in dreams of delight
Away back to the spot where I first saw the light
To the days of my childhood ere I ever did roam
From that cosy thatched cottage - my old mountain home.

What joy and what gladness in that old home we knew
With our loving parents so kind and so true
Through their love for each other God's blessings did come
To that cosy thatched cottage - my old mountain home.

By the fireside we gathered as Jack Frost tried in vain
Through the hot leaping flames a bold entrance to gain
As Dad told fairy stories or recited a poem
In that cosy thatched cottage - my old mountain home.

The old patriot songs in his charming sweet voice
Brought us many pleasures our hearts to rejoice
Sadly we had to wander across o'er the foam
From that cosy thatched cottage - my old mountain home.

Sadder still is the fact that that home is no more
Now a derelict sight without windows or door
There a welcome awaited everyone that did roam
To that cosy thatched cottage- my old mountain home.

Still in fancy I hear the click of the latch
As a neighbour entered 'neath the roof of brown thatch
Praying "God save all here" on the old threshold stone
Of that cosy thatched cottage - my old mountain home.

All the world I'd give there once more to partake
Of the nice griddle bread my fond mother did bake
And the fine floury spuds with a taste of their own
In that cosy thatched cottage - my old mountain home.

To spend the long nights of the winter we sat round the blazing turf fire
As the neighbours all congregated of their company we never would tire.
As they recalled to us fairy stories and many the weird ghostly tale
Which made us feel frightened and nervous in the dark by the banks of the Gale.

There in Kelly's hall in the village we danced a good polka and reel
As we spun like a top with our colleens, such joy in our hearts we did feel.
Then when the dances had ended away with our sweethearts we'd stale
To enjoy a session of courting in the barns by the banks of the gale.

Alas, for those days I am sighing, those days I shall never see more
My heart is sick with a longing, a longing for those dear days of yore.
For Athea and its kind-hearted people where good humour doth always prevail
And the air is so wholesome and fragrant along by the banks of the Gale.

Railway Lines to Ardagh

She:

You are the man I heard 'em saying
That killed my goat with your auld train
Why did you kill her? Come explain
On the railway lines to Ardagh.

He:

I'm sorry to say 'twas me alright
That killed your little goat last night
But you know damn well on the track he had no right
On the railway lines to Ardagh.

She:

'Tis you my man that is to blame
Why didn't you pull up your train?
My poor little goat that had milk like crame
You killed on the railway lines to Ardagh.

He:

'Tis there my good woman you are wrong
You know my train is powerful strong
How could I halt her flying along
The railway lines to Ardagh.

She:

Your blooming train can scarcely hoot
Auld smokey hole of ash and soot.
'Twill very soon be off the route
Of the railways lines to Ardagh.

He:

Yerra don't mind my train but tell me this
You're gamey looking that's what 'tis
Maybe you'd give me one auld kiss
On the railway lines to Ardagh.

She:

Keep out from me you blasted rogue
The cheek of you you gamalogue
I'll flatten you with my citeóg
On the railway lines to Ardagh.

He:

There's no need for you to shout or roar
I kissed far nicer girls than you before
And most of them came back for more
On the railway lines to Ardagh.

She:

I'd like my job then kissing you
I'd be short-taken for a thing to do
With a puss on you like a Kerry blue
On the railway lines to Ardagh.

He:

A Kerry blue's puss would be tastier than your mouth
'Twould fit in well with your frozen snout
I think when beauty came it passed you out
On the railway lines to Ardagh.

She:

You insulting tramp I'll let you see
That I will sue the company
And for my goat they'll pay me
On the railway lines to Ardagh

He:

Against you Ma'am they have the law
For yourself or your goat they care a straw
So you might as well now close your jaw
On the railway lines to Ardagh.

She:

Close my jaw indeed I will
Not until myself you'll kill
May the Devil roast your arse in hell
From the railway lines to Ardagh.

Lovely Clounleharde

My memories fly to days gone by when a gorsoon I did roam
O'er hill and dale, through glen and vale around my native home.
The cheerful ways of those dear days were not by sorrow marred,
No care or woe we then did know in lovely Clounleharde.

With schoolmates gay I went my way across the meadows green.
In summertime when the sun did shine and wild birds sang serene,
Their nests to find we were inclined and time did disregard,
Till the Master's ire we put on fire when late in Clounleharde.

With fork in hand we tried to land the twisting slippery eel,
With joyous pranks on the river banks many happy hours did steal.
There oft' of yore with school hours o'er upon the green clad sward
With hearts so light oft' 'till the night we played in Clounleharde.

There in my teens with the sweet colleens we often took the floor,
In the local hall where crowds did call ere emigration hit our shore
But now, alas, each lad and lass on outgoing ships are carred,
And bound like me across the sea from lovely Clounleharde.

Some day again if God ordains the Atlantic I'll recross,
To my native home from across the foam and seek an Irish lass,
There as my bride by the mountainside united by the Lord,
We'll settle down beside Bricktown in lovely Clounleharde,

Home in the Mountain

There's a tree in the mountain when on it I gaze
It takes back my memory to the sweet yesterdays
When as innocent children we gaily did play
Round that home in the mountain four miles from Athea

Barefoot we rambled o'er bogland and mead
Our hearts full of pleasure quite happy indeed
As we listened to the corncrake at the close of the day
Near that home in the mountain four miles from Athea

As we passed o'er the moorland quietly looking beneath
We saw the grouse hatching in her nest in the heath
While the curlew was calling in a shrill plaintive way
Near that home in the mountain four miles from Athea

In the twilight shadows with jam crocks in our hands
We picked in abundance the luscious freáchans
And played hide-and-seek round the neat cocks of hay
Near that home in the mountain four miles from Athea

How we children enjoyed the soft liquid peat
Ooze up 'tween our toes from the soft bog underneath
As we watched tiny tadpoles go squirting away
Near that home in the mountain four miles from Athea

Those days are long gone but their memories remain
Oh! what would I give to live them o'er again
Please God we will meet up in Heaven some day
O'er that home in the mountain four miles from Athea

Electric Love

There lived two old ladies far in from the road
In their simple old fashioned way
With no thought of the world and its modern code
And the up to date things of today
With their big open turf fire, their skillet and pot
And their snuffbox so cherished and brown
So peaceful and quiet and content with their lot
Far away from the din of the town.

They decided one day when the Lord called away
Their two loving parents together
That nothing would separate Mary and Kate
They'd work hand in hand with each other
And so the years went, their hearts quite content
Through sunshine rain and all weather
Wherever Mary was seen there too was Kateen
Working hand in hand with each other.

And by their fireside so warm and bright
Their hearts as light as a feather
Sat Katie and Mary as happy as Larry
Having their pinch of snuff there together
But their peace was disturbed when an ESB man called
Asking the ladies to agree
To sign a form to link up their house
And he'd bring in electricity.

Mary:
"'Electercitee' is a thing we don't want
You can leave it abroad of the door
We wouldn't touch that old thing we know nothing about
It could stretch us out dead on the floor
'Tis only the other day a man was telling me

His wife was working with that
It gave her a shock that put out her backbone
And she's since lying down on her flat."

ESB Man:
"You have nothing to fear I assure you of that
'Tis all as simple as dip
There's a switch on the wall when you want the light on
With your finger just give it a tip
'Twill boil up a pot, 'twill iron your clothes
A kettle 'twill boil in a minute
All you need do is just plug it in
Quite simple there's nothing in it."

Katie:
"Wisha Mary did you listen and hear what he said
As to cod us I'm sure he's not able
Does he think we believe you could boil a pot on the hob
With a knob on the wall near the table?"

Mary:
"Anyway, Katie 'tis a dangerous affair
To touch it we never would venture
How often as you know did we patch our old knickers
With only the light of a splinter.
You may say we'll hold on to our parafin lamp
And keep that old thing at a distance
If lightening came with all them wires round the house
'Twould blow us clane out of existence!
I assure you, kind Sir, if the burner was cleaned
We'd have light good enough here to suit us
The Lord knows in these times we have trouble enough
Without you coming to electeracute us!"

ESB Man:
"Now 'tis all very fine to be talking like that
But suppose now, we'll view it this way
I know very well two fine girls like you
Will join up in wedlock some day.
And bring in a man to this nice little home
Where everything is so neat and so bright
When he'd sit down at night the paper to read
He'd love to have electric light.
And maybe at night if the baby was cross
With the cold affecting its feet
Wouldn't it be far easier than lighting a fire
To turn on the electric heat?"

Mary:
"Now you're joking in earnest I know by your eye
For you know that we're left on the shelf."

ESB Man:
"I don't but I know ye're too hard to be pleased
If I stood a chance I'd propose myself!"

Katie:
"You're an awful old joker but anyway my man
Give me that form you brought in."

Mary:
"Go aisy now Katie and leave it to me
I'm better than you at the pen!"

Katie:
"Wisha Mary indeed what boasting you have
Is it long 'til we have it, my man
Maybe when we get it you'll come back again
And stay with me to turn it on".

ESB Man:
"There's nothing on earth I'd like better than that
I've prayed every day of my life
To get a nice little homestead like this
And one such as you for a wife.
Therefore little maidens I'll be counting the days
Til the current your house they will bring
Then round here I'll steer to live with you here
And then wedding bells they will ring
So goodbye for the present the boss is in the car
And he told me not to delay
Although I'm reluctant I now must be going
But I'll be looking out for that day."

Katie:
"Goodbye my old darling I hope 'twon't be long
'til you'll be returning to me."

Mary:
"Shah! 'Goodbye my old darling' the thought makes me smile
For 'tis I that will have him Katie, you'll see."
In due time the house was linked up
Switch plug and meter installed
Bulbs in position, the whole lot in place
But the man that had promised never called.
Two months later another man came along
And called in the meter to read
The units registered on the meter thereon
Caused him to be surprised indeed.
He enquired of the ladies if 'twas working alright
For they seemed to have burnt no units at all.
"Faith, 'tis working alright Sir, we turns it on
While we're putting oil in the lamp on the wall!"

Fiona the Physiotherapist

When I with the pain of arthritis unfortunately was laid low
I was advised for treatment to a physiotherapist to go
They told me there was no one better so I did enlist
In the hope of getting great relief from Fiona the Physiotherapist

She was waiting there inside the door as I entered in
She said "Are you Paddy Faley? Strip in the bed there to the skin"
She drew the curtains round the end and
'tis one date I'd have missed
If I knew what lay before me with Fiona the Physiotherapist

"Stretch your left hand out," she said,
"and then stretch out your right
Put your hands up o'er your head and then down by your side".
The exercise was painful but she sternly did insist
My groans were music to the ears of Fiona the Physiotherapist

Then she took my head between her hands and with an iron grip
She nearly pulled it from my shoulders she gave it such a whip
She then spun it completely round with the strength of her strong
wrist
And I dreaded what she would do next - Fiona the Physiotherapist

When I was inclined to give up she said, "Instructions take from me
Turn over there in the bed and stretch out on your tummy".
She was about to do something untold that would put me out of tune
So she blinded me with opaque blue glasses
so I couldn't see what she was doing.
"Oh God in Heaven" I prayed, "Grant me this one request
Save me from the awful torture of Fiona the Physiotherapist."

With her two knees upon my back she showed me no remorse
As she bruised every inch of me from my poll down to my arse
With the excruciating pain I had no choice but to roar and grin
But down through the blooming mattress
she pushed my nose and chin

But I'm glad to say I did not give up and
for further treatment I did go
And the good that I gained from it, 'tis only now I know
For my arthritis pains have greatly eased
and I can rock and roll and twist
But I'll not be in any hurry back to Fiona the Physiotherapist.

Fond Memories

*This song won 1st place in the Limerick Co. Fleadh 2003 for newly
composed Ballads sung by John O'Riordan, Granagh
(Written after I visited the grave
on the 25th anniversary of my wife's death)*

How I wish that you could speak
to me from out your bed of clay
As I kneel upon your grave here in Templeathea
I know my wishes can't be granted for such is death alas
But, somehow I feel you're listening as I weed away the grass.

I'm gazing on the tombstone that denotes where you lie
As my mind goes madly chasing back to happy days gone by
Through ten happy years of wedded bliss
that only Heaven could share
As I gazed upon your gentle smiling face
as your laughter filled the air.

To our happy days of courtship I am travelling back again
As our love for each other grew as God did so ordain
When we two were joined together in the year of '52
In that holy church in 'Glantine where
we pledged that we'd be true.

We shared the happy years that passed
as the children came along
With your wise nature guiding them always
in your humourous mind a song
As your industrious little fingers were working in top gear
Knitting, washing, sewing and baking
as you kept them in good cheer.
Five and twenty years have passed
since your body here was laid

Beneath this mound of mouldering clay
when death forced us to separate
But your memory will never die
How can it fade away?
When your image in your daughters
I'm looking on every day.

Great happiness they've brought to me
and their children are bringing too
Renewing in my memory the days I spent with you
For them to God I'm thankful for their merry company
But you alone can fill the chair that by my fire I see.

Sometimes when I feel down and out or filled with loneliness
I pour out my woes to you to relieve me of distress
I'm sure you come to my rescue as my courage I regain
To fulfil my mission here on earth until we meet again.

How long I'll be waiting for that certain day to come
Is in the hands of the God above to call my soul back home
Hoping when that call will come,
death for me will bring no fears
But the joy of our first meeting
after all those absent years.

I tried to scrape off the burned crusts to
make it edible for the children and my wife
But I only broke the handle of a Sheffield Stainless knife.
I cursed and prayed together – I was nearly off my head
I had to throw out the homemade loaf and go for Bakery bread.

Then she informed me that she was longing for a fry
She told me how I'd cook it and so I said I'd try
My fry was going grand in top gear 'twould delight the heart of man
'Twas singing like a fiddle and dancing in the pan.
But when I poured in some water to make 'dip' out of the grease
The whole thing then exploded and the frying pan went ablaze.

I grabbed the burning frying pan and for the door did wheel
The dog he came before me and I was pitched head o'er heel
Hot grease was splashed all o'er me as my forehead hit the floor
The dog, roaring with a scalded arse, out through the window tore!

That evening the children from school came rushing in
I couldn't hear my ears with them, such a racket and a din
Quarrelling over this and that – I never heard such rows
Or why did they wait to pick this day to go mad around the house.
They were calling for their dinner and with hunger they did shout
When I went to boil the kettle the fire it had gone out!

When at last the night came on and the children did retire
I sat down exhausted on my chair beside the fire
I took up the daily paper to read it for a while
But soon I was in darkness the lamp ran out of oil.

I caught the globe it was red hot and God forgive me I did curse it
For at that very minute I was praying to God to kick the bucket
I shook my hand with the burning pain and
from the wife there came a scream
As she heard her fire proof Pyrex globe
land on the floor in smithereens.

Now she was beseeching God and His Blessed and Holy Mother
To get her out of bed while there was something left together
She said "Go there to the dresser, behind the dishes
and you'll find a candle there
There's one left over after Christmas
and mind don't break the ware!"

Well I am one cursed man wherever there's another
For I broke a China Vase – a wedding present from her mother!
Another lecture from the bed saying "Aren't you an awful curse
Instead of you improving you're going from bad to worse
No one in the world knows what I am going through
Or how did the good God ever splice me to
an awkward fool like you!"

Anyway I lit up my candle and the light was not so clear
To have it close by me I placed it on the range I was sitting near
I then read on my paper 'til the light grew dim and strange
When I looked there was my candle like a pancake on the range!

Before I did more harm for the bed I then did race
But I struck my toe against the po and spilled it round the place
As long as I live I won't forget the lecturing she gave to me
The story wouldn't be so bad if she was wasn't suffering from a bad
dose of diarrhoea!

After mopping up I got into bed and was nice and warm there
When I heard a cry of anguish from a child in bed upstairs
Saying "Dad, come up quick. I think I'm going to puke!"
To comfort her I had to hop out from my warm nook.

Probing in the darkness up the stairway I did go
I struck my foot against the step and disjointed my big toe
When again I had got into bed under the warm clothes
With aching head and painful toe I had started off to doze.

The dog he started barking and she woke me with a roar
Saying "As sure as God, Paddy, that's the fox.
Did you close the fowlhouse door?"
To add to my misery there I was again
Running out to close it and I naked to the skin.

I returned from the henhouse, my backside as cold as clay
The frost had froze my thighs and toes and
perished what I won't say.
I squeezed in beside her for the heat – I was like a walking corpse
She said " Keep out from me you icicle
or you'll give me the relapse!"

But I won't be caught again for I know what I'll do
The very first sneeze I hear out of her – I'll start sneezing too!

Modern Love

"Oh, Mary dear you've won my heart and my life I'd give now for your sake
Together with my land and cattle for if you leave me my heart will break
So Darling, do not leave me pining, to be my bride you will agree
And we'll live together content and happy like my parents did in Turraree."

"Oh Johnny darling, I'll not leave you pining if you prove to me you love me so
I'd be delighted to share your dwelling and in married life with you to go.
Then you won't refuse one request I ask you a nice new car you'll get for me,
For of course you know now times are different to what they were in Turraree."

"You'll want no motor Mary darling for I've a lively pony and trap
Who'd hold his own with any motor as he hits the road going tap, tap, tap.
'Twas in that trap on his wedding morning my father drove like a Lord or Squire
An 'tis as good today if it isn't better for I exchanged the bands for rubber tyres."

"Oh Johnny dear you would not risk my life thus, in the tar roads now he'd surely slip
With the fall of ground through Ballyhahill he was bound to tumble, he'd catch no grip.
Then you'd never forget, 'twould be next to murder when on the road there I would be thrown
What a state you'd be in when then you'd find me with a broken skull or a cracked backbone."

"In that pony and trap you'd be as safe as could be he'd never falter you can be sure of it,
For on his shoes there fixed securely are four new studs by our local smith.
You know my love if there was any danger I wouldn't risk your life on the slippery tar
I think the money would yield more profit in any other investment than a motor car."

"Now Johnny dear, there's no good in hoarding if you love me so why my request refuse
Since you offered your life, give me your bank book and I'll put the money to good use.
My love for you will then grow stronger as you sit beside me in a posh new car,
And we'll enjoy life with a throw of brandy as we drive to places near and far."

"I think young lady, you are a wastrel and soon in my pocket you'd have a hole
My bank account would soon diminish and I'd find myself thrown on the dole.
Then you'd hoist your sails and fly to England and leave the children with me to mind,
So I'm thinking now ere that thing happens you can go your road and I'll change my mind."

"You grey haired miser I now am wiser you want my love for the pig's trough
But you can be certain and sure Sir, no child of yours in the cradle would I ever rock.
For your land and cattle I don't give a rattle they'd never coax me you to wed,
Your cows and reactors would drive me crackers and in the mental I'd find my bed.

For your trap and pony you'll find some apeish Joany, from your pigs
and cowdung I'll keep far out
The man to win my heart and hand in wedlock is a man with a motor-
car drinking pints of stout."

My Home in Athea

Won 1st place in Fleadh Ceoil Limerick newly composed ballads in 2002

I've travelled far far from the land of my birth
And been to many places all over the earth
But my heart stayed behind where I first saw the day
With my kindly neighbours in my home in Athea.

Back where the people are courteous and kind
And your face is kissed by the soft April wind
And the cuckoo is calling to welcome the May
Amid peaceful surroundings in my home in Athea.

The lark in the blue sky whistles a tune
To cheer up our hearts in the sweet month of June
From twilight the corncrake keeps craking away
What memories they bring of my home in Athea.

My heart it is aching to go back once more
And join my companions on the old dancing floor
And tune up my fiddle a polka to play
To get them all going in my home in Athea.

Now the fiddle hangs silent and mute on the wall
In the land of the stranger where no neighbours call
My old feeble fingers no longer can play
As they once used to do in my home in Athea.

Now old and alone my mind wanders back
To the good times we had with the fun and the craic
My wandering life has brought me nothing today
And I'm constantly sighing for my home in Athea.

My days are now numbered and I'm ready to go
When God calls my soul from this valley below
To enjoy my Heaven for ever and aye
And meet up with my friends from my home in Athea.

My old Raleigh Bike

This world is full of commotion like it never witnessed before,
The people are rolling in riches with motors lined up at each door.
There's a feverish desire for speeding, many cars are built for the like,
But while they are smashing all records give me my old Raleigh bike.

It takes me to Beale and Kilteery, Ballybunion and Killarney so green,
Abbeyfeale, Mountcollins and 'Glantine, where I courted my darling
colleen,
I have no bother in starting, no dirty plugs that won't strike,
And you'll never hear any back-firing from the exhaust of my old
Raleigh bike.

I have no fear of the Garda, no tax disc need I ever show,
I need no insurance cover or a driving test undergo,
Let CIE go bust in the morning or the whole damn lot go on strike,
While planes, trains and buses are stranded I have my old Raleigh
bike.

I have no stops to get petrol and Caltex gets none of my dough,
It keeps me as fit as a fiddle, but for it I'd be stiff long ago,
You can call me an old-fashioned timer or anything else that you like,
But I'm always as happy as Larry when riding my old Raleigh bike.

When I was living in Glasha that bike carried many a load,
Bags and bags of provisions to the house from the old County road,
Bags of cement and lime to make mortar, spades, shovels, a scythe,
and a pike,
'Twas as good as a Ferguson tractor, my famous old Raleigh bike.

I kept a few cows and I milked them and that bike was my creamery
car,
As I struck off every morning with my tankard tied onto the bar,
My children to Mass on a Sunday never the road had to hike,
For four of us travelled together all on top of my old Raleigh bike.

Rahilly's Glen

In a quiet spot in Toureendonnell, Athea, there is a place known as Rahillys Glen. This place is now owned by James Kiely; Knocknagorna. At present it is not remote but there was a time before the road leading from Knocknagorna by Knocknaclugga was laid down and the road south of this place by Templeathea, Fairy Street and 'Slienteragh' was not in existence.

At that time this particular spot in Toureendonnell was very remote and isolated from the general public. Here there dwelt a family by the name of Rahilly - three men and a woman. They became noted robbers as it turned out to be. Often in my childhood I heard my father tell of their activities in the neighbourhood but, unfortunately, I did not retain all of his knowledge concerning their exploits and the history of their crimes.

However, during a conversation with old Mike Dineen (RIP.) of Knocknagorna some years ago he recalled for me an account of those robbers that had been related to him by Mrs. Con O'Sullivan who owned the shop near the bridge in Athea. She was one of the O'Connells from Glenbawn, Ballyhahill.

Rahilly's house, she said, was a long crudely built construction up against the steep face of the cliff. There were three strong roughlooking long-bearded men who kept aloof, not mixing or conversing with the other natives.

There was also a woman but, contrary to the men, she travelled through the locality visiting houses but her main interest was spotting where there would be sheep or fowl or other spoil for the men to steal in one of their clever raids.

These robbers were operating for a long period without being caught in the act or suspected, but as the saying goes "as long as the fox runs he'll be caught". It happened one night as the snow was falling, the robbers raided the farm of O'Connell in Glenbawn (the father of the above-mentioned Mrs. O'Sullivan) and the next door farm of Mr. Joyce who lived where Roger Behane later owned and later still owned by John Leahy who married Roger's daughter, Eileen. During the snowstorm they stole sheep but they were not gone very far from the farms when the snow suddenly ceased falling. The owners of the stolen sheep tracked the robbers in the snow to their homestead. On gazing in quietly through the small window they saw the robbers who were actually in the act of skinning the sheep and refreshing themselves with bowls of hot soup.

Messrs. Joyce and O'Connell proceeded to the police station in Newcastle West. The police quickly arrived at the house and charged the inmates. The robbers were tried, convicted and sentenced to Van Diemen's land. I heard my father say that the police, in order to shame them and deter others from stealing, marched them through Athea with a piece of meat tied to their backs.

Buried beside their house were found bags of feathers from stolen geese and hides of sheep and from the inside of the house an underground drain ran, taking the blood of slaughtered animals to the nearby river.

Where the Rahillys came from to take up their abode in this particular place no one seemed to know but we do know that no one of the name is living in the locality now but the place is still known as Rahilly's Glen.

The Shakey

I witnessed a phenomenal incident in the month of May in 1984. It was in the area of virgin bogland known as "The Shakey" east of Clounleharde along the Kerryline. It aparently did not get that name without a reason. It had been taken over by a company for planting and, as it happened, I was working with the Council on the roadway nearby when the first machine entered to prepare for the planting of the trees. It was a heavy machine on tracks.

The driver had travelled sixty yards or so when the machine started to sink. He jumped off and with great presence of mind attached a strong steel rope to it. Dumbfounded he stood whilst it sank deeper and deeper into the soft peat until eventually it had disappeared.

People in the neighbourhood, hearing of the event, gathered to look at this unusual happening. There it remained for a couple of days whilst the owners discussed, wracked their brains and consulted others about ways and means of rescuing the machine from the hidden depths.

A few days afterwards a rescue gang arrived with different types of very heavy machines which they attached together directly across the road from the sunken vehicle. A strong pulley rope was then attached to a pulley wheel and the tugging began. The rope cut itself into the bog when it took the strain but, after a while, we saw heaving on the surface as the machine began to be towed underneath the ground, which would swell up overhead, like a wave, as it passed and fall back into place again. Thus the tugging went on until the machine started to appear like a submarine on reaching the sound ground near the roadway. Thus the machine was rescued.

As I said this bogland was not called "The Shakey" without earning the name. All the stories, which we thought were only myths, that we heard from the old folk about cattle disappearing without a trace – yes, human beings too – losing their lives in this area, has now been proved true. No man in his senses, hearing this incident would venture working on this fearsome ground.

On the 75th Birthday
of Radio Eireann

I was just at the age of reason when Radio Éireann came on
Bringing great excitement to the life of everyone
Some things fresh in my memory though many long years have passed
I remember well the joy I got from The Kennedys of Castleross.

Then we had Music for Middlebrows with famous Des Keogh
And Rory O'Connor dancing on the floor taken by Din Joe
Una Collins, Seán O Siochain, Martin Dempsey and Joe Lynch
Their melodious voices never left my memory since.

To raise up my spirits and my heart fill with delight
I listened to the Ceilí House and Ballad Maker Saturday night
Ciarán MacMathúna through the country travelled all around
To bring us his recordings that in all parts he found

Donncha O Dulaing kept on walking with untiring feet
Telling us of his exploits and the people he did meet
Unequalled Eamon Kelly told of his Father's Time
And Eamon Keane recited his verses so sublime.

Leo Rowsome on his pipes the cockles of your heart would stir
Where would you find a better singer than Bridie Gallagher
From Croke Park every Sunday excitement filled the air
With thirty players doing their best to keep pace with Micheál O Hehir.

Delia Murphy another singer whose equals are few
Two more I well remember, Larry Gogan and Liam O Murchú
How could I forget Paddy Crosbie and his School Around The Corner
And I often won a guinea on John O Donovan's Dear Sir or Madam.

If I wanted to increase my knowledge and test my tired brain
I could listen to 20 Questions with learned Joe Linnane
These are just some memories of seventy-five years gone by
Listening to Radio Eireann and the good times I enjoyed.

My Home in Sweet Lyrecrompane

Far away from my homeland in Kerry
I've been for a number of years
Although I'm contented and happy
My memory it fondly adheres
To that dear little spot by the Sméarla
Where I first saw the light of the dawn
And spent the sweet days of my childhood
In my home in sweet Lyrecrompane.

Oh dear Lyre I can never forget you
No matter how long I'm away
In my mind you're as fresh as a daisy
Or the wind blowing in from the bay.
When Ireland was fighting for freedom
To her colours her true sons were drawn
And fought for the freedom of Ireland
And their homes in sweet Lyrecrompane.

The music and song at the crossroads
I can still hear so clearly today
As in fancy my mind often wanders
To those days gone so far far away.
There on the flag floor in the kitchen
We often danced until dawn

God be with the dear days of my childhood
In my home in sweet Lyrecrompane.

In dreams I am sometimes awakened
By the Sméarla that flows there beyond
Where I often fished in its waters
And fine catches of salmon did land
Those days are now gone forever
All the wealth of the world I'd pawn
If I could get them back and return
As a gorsoon to sweet Lyrecrompane.

The Post-Boxes at the Road

God be with the good old days when Michéal the Postman came
To deliver the letters at our doors, very trustworthy at that same
How glad we were to see him for all the news he'd bring
Of local happenings roundabout within our kith and kin.

He'd tell us of all those with their harvest done and their turf carted
home
Of emigrants left the district and those returned from oe'r the foam
In our districts we miss him now. 'An Post' has changed the code
The letters are only delivered now to their boxes at the road.

Micheal would tell us of forthcoming weddings and those who
engaged had got
Of courting couples who were going strong and those of 'em who
were not
Of newborn babies we were informed and expectant mothers too
Of those pubs raided after hours when the Gardai their rounds would
do

All new residents to the Parish were greeted by Micheal
Who instructed them in local ways when to their house he'd call
He made them all feel much at home and were to them a friend
In every way he possibly could, a helping hand he'd lend
We'd be told where the dangerous potholes were
Of it he'd make a note

We get no information now from the boxes at the road.
In this place where daily papers we may not receive at all
Of every death and funeral we'd be informed of by Micheal
'You won't miss the water 'til the well runs dry'
Oh what a truthful quote
'Tis vividly brought home to us in the post boxes at the road

I remember many years ago when postal stamps were just two pence each
A postman on his bicycle every home would reach
How is it now with increased rate and postal vans to booth
They can't afford to travel further than the boxes at the road.

To old aged people living alone, the postman was a boon
If they needed assistance he'd relate it quick and soon
And help to them soon found its way to their remote abode
Their communication line is cut off now with the boxes at the road.

Shy Bachelor

Mother:
"It's about time now John that you got married
I'm afraid too long now you have tarried
The next thing is that I'll be buried
Before you'll bring in a wife."

Son
"Indeed you won't you're not that old
You're well able to fight and scold
Maybe next year now when I'll get bold
I'll settle down in life."

Mother
"Ah 'tis next year with you for the last forty years
You often drive me into tears
If you let it go much longer I have great fears
You'll get no woman at all."

Son
"If I don't itself mother I can pull away
All the girls are not Saints today
Some can hardly make a drop of tay
They'd drive me up the wall."

Mother
"Keep talking like that and you'll be alright
When I'm gone you'll get a fright
Then the County Home will be your plight
When no one about you cares.
Pity for bachelors no one can find
Their heads go grey and they gets quare in the mind
Having no children to take their place behind
Or offer for them a prayer."

Son

"Now mother I know a few men that wed
And no hair at all was left on their head
There were lumps from the poker there instead
And blisters from boiled water.
They got women who would drink and smoke
And in no time they had them broke
God help us mother 'tis no joke
To bring in another man's daughter."

Mother

"Tis true for the Holy Fathers when they did call
That bachelors had no sense at all
Looking at their shadows on the wall
Ould idiots and amadáns
With lonesome faces then they'll go
With their long pipes and their Bendigo
May the devil smoke 'em down below
On a fire of black ciaráns"

Son

"Anyway there's no woman here to be found
Over to England they all are bound
They're wild to land on a foreign ground
The Devil wouldn't please 'em."

Mother

"'Tis not their fault John 'tis not I say
They're perfectly right to go away
When the cowardly men we have here today
Won't court or kiss or squeeze 'em.
Can't you go and get married like your father, John
There is no fear at all that you'll get on
You'll have comfort in bed when the frost comes on
And she'll keep you out of danger."

Son

"Here now mother that will do
Marriage is a thing I could not go through
'Twas different with Dad he married you
But you want me to marry a stranger!"

Get Back to the Spud
and the Spade

Buttermilk and potatoes was our forefathers diet.
With bacon and cabbage and brown bread not white,
With yalla meal gruel their sound bellies they filled,
No blood pressure or arthritis as their gardens they tilled.

They grew up strong and healthy, no pains or backache,
No Andrews or tablets did they need to take,
No corns or bunions, they walked miles and miles,
To Mass and to fairs their faces full of smiles.

Some attended Mass in their turns, they shared the same suit,
With no heels in their socks in their strong hobnailed boots,
Yet their song light and gay ascended in the air like a rocket,
With a flour bag for a shirt and not a bob in their pocket.

Yet they were affectionate and kind, always ready to share,
Their help with a neighbour who needed their care,
And any poor traveller caught out in the night,
Was welcome to a place by their homely fireside.

Today in old Ireland 'tis a different scene,
And great changes have come in our Isle of Green,
The times for our people were never as good.
With all kinds of dainties and a variety of food.

No walking, no working, we have buses and cars,
To take us to Mass and to the lounge bars,
Yet in the midst of all luxuries we all seem out of tune,
Groaning and moaning night, morning and noon.

Our bones are all aching, our bodies all ills,
We can't stand, we can't walk, we can't pee without pills,
The doctors are thriving from our visits and moans,
And the chemists enlarging their staff and their homes.

Let us get back digging in our gardens once more,
To produce fresh wholesome food and our tinned food ignore,
Then of all the tablets we soon will be rid,
And we'll sing and enjoy life as our forefathers did.

The Sweet Kerryline

There's a dear little spot that's calling me home
From this land where in exile I stray
And no peace of mind will I ever find
'till again I'll go back there some day
By its neat shady nooks and its quiet rippling brook
Where I sported with rod and with line
Along by the river that haunts me forever
That flows by the sweet Kerryline.

The pain of the exile is breaking my heart
And my thoughts are forever at home
In the land of my birth that's the fairest on earth
And that road there where oft' I did roam.
By its hedgerows calm shade with a pretty fair maid
As the moonbeams around us did shine
And the Heavens above seem to pour down with their love
Along by the sweet Kerryline.

Oh beautiful spot so enchanting thy scenes
That nature did kindly bestow
Your hillside so green and charming valleys between
That would equal the Gap of Dunloe
Now declared far and wide as Erin's great pride
But if itself and lakes were all mine
I'd give the whole lot and all the States here with that
For one stroll on the sweet Kerryline.

There in the morning with the sunshine adorning
The linnet and blackbird do sing
And the thrush and the lark are up with the dark
To welcome the fragrance of spring
Your brain it is kissed with the May morning mist
Like a feeling of something divine

And wild flowers so gay are all painting the way
Alone by the sweet Kerryline.

In the summertime too the welcome cuckoo
Her own name she'll fondly repeat
As the soft balmy breeze steals on through the trees
To cool off the hot noonday heat
There are bees buzzing by and the bright butterfly
And the sweet scented heather like wine
And the fields of rich corn are there to adorn
The slopes of the sweet Kerryline.

In the twilight of Autumn, Direen's colleens it brought 'em
With young lads and ladies from Blaine
And Glasha likewise and gay Turraree boys
Whose found memories I will always retain
Sweet colleens from Knockdown, Glenbawn and Bricktown
All together in Glenagragra they'd join
In a sight so serene to dance on the green
By the side of sweet Kerryline.

Towards the close of the year when wren parties appear
'Tis there you'll get many a thrill
With the gay spirit flying with music and wine
All worries and frowns it would kill
With hornpipes and reel, step dancing and wheel
Would keep going 'till daylight would shine
Oh I wish I was there those joys for to share
With my friends on the sweet Kerryline.

Weeping Mother Erin
Written in the 1960's

Oh weeping mother Erin must thou always be in tears
With a heart so full of anguish down through the countless years
As tyrants and invaders came and pierced thy loving brow
But never mother Erin were thou grieved as thou art now
To see your sons and daughters all going across the main
Those children whom you cherished you may never see again
With sympathy dear mother my tears and yours are mingling
To see a once proud Irish race ever ever dwindling.

Oh Mother how you suffered to defend your faith and home
Against cruel forms of a torment from
the enemy o'er the foam
Then you had your sons and daughters working
hand in hand with you
Ever eager ever-ready to help you Róisin Dubh.
It must cause your heart great sorrow dear mother now to see
Your noble Irish children forced to work with your enemy
Who tortured you, who beggared you, and cut you into two
And leave you here still bleeding with no sympathy for you.

Is there any way dear mother we can dispel all this distress
Shall our voices ever an echo be crying in the wilderness
While the last drops of your precious blood
are being sucked out of your veins
By departing loads of emigrants in ships and aeroplanes
For years in hope you waited now with despair you're sighing
As you see more British troops sent in to reinforce the borderline
The outlook is gloomy for you dear mother Erin

For everything that you hold dear I see them disappearing
Your grand old Irish customs are now regarded droll
Your own traditional dancing is replaced by rock and roll
Your fairy forts and leprechauns with your Gaelic are now dying
'Tis no wonder. Who can blame you,
poor old mother that you're crying?

Yielding's Waterfall
Written in 1965

If you're ever in West Limerick come on to Glenastar,
'Tis at the west of Ardagh closeby the river Daar,
When you'll come to see it once, time and again you'll call,
For your heart it will be captured by Yielding's Waterfall.

As you admire the scenery you'll hear the fragrant breeze.
Go singing through the valley so picturesque with trees.
'Tis like a bit of Heaven where peace reigns over all,
The angels seem to hover 'round Yielding's Waterfall.

The place looks so romantic 'twill fill your heart with love,
As you walk its flowery pathways beside the shady grove,
You'll linger there the whole day long
'til night's dark shadows fall,
And even then you're loath to go from Yielding's Waterfall.

There from the road above it you can view the countryside.
For leagues and leagues onto the east, away o'er Galtee's side,
So come and see this grandeur,
you're welcome when you call,
Tis with a sigh you'll say goodbye to Yielding's Waterfall.

It brought back home the wanderer from out the foreign land,
Who thought he could forget it in cities bright and grand,
When its homely voice appealed he answered to the call,
For he knew that he would pine away from Yielding's Waterfall.

The Vales of Sweet Dirreen

More worthy poets of other days have sung thy praises oh lovely plain
And your sun-kissed slopes extending from the county bounds to the cross of Blaine
Again thy grandeur calls forth in song the pleasant thoughts on your verdant green
As with mind enraptured I gaze upon
The lovely vales of Sweet Dirreen

Your murmuring brook through the picturesque valley
Its flower decked banks my eyes do trail
As by hazel covert and flagstone quarry
It goes on singing to the winding Gale
As if in chorus the skylark tuning and the blackbird whistling his notes serene
And from the hazel bough the thrushes warbling
reverberates through Sweet Dirreen

Nature's beauty is freely lavished
In your wooded dells and shady glens
And your air so wholesome with fragrance flavoured
With beauteous wild flowers growing therein
Your jovial people are a treat to meet them
no gloomy faces there will be seen
No thoughts of sorrow the mind can follow
in the carefree vales of Sweet Dirreen

Your vales inspired into religious orders
Your modest daughters with talents rare
Who in convents here and across the waters
are serving God in holy prayer
There you bred the Vaughans the champion dancers
whose pleasant manner would charm the Queen
The Lynch musicians, the poet Jerr Histon
and the Aherne athletes in Sweet Dirreen

From the vales of beauty to a patriot's duty
your sons stepped forward in '21
When their mother bleeding her cries unheeding
was being molested by the Black and Tan
From your slopes and valleys your heroes rallied
and fought side-by-side to uphold the green
To no foreign crown would they bow down
in the lovely vales of Sweet Dirreen

If we choose to travel south by Croom on to famed Bruree
And to Kilmallock's famous walls steeped in history
Neath the shadow of the Galtees
as by the border we drive along
We pass scenic Ballylanders, Elton and Knocklong.

Hospital, Kilteely and Pallasgreen steeped in ancient lore
And neath Slieve Felim mountains lies Doon and Cappamore
Back by Brittas and Boher our pleasant way we'll wend
Again to the city of the Treaty Stone at our journey's end.

Why Can't We Whistle Now

Why has all the whistling ceased we heard for many a year
Then every Irish heart was glad
and the mind full of good cheer
Then kindly neighbours had time to chat
In the good old days gone by
And their merry lips oft' whistled as the lark up in the sky.
Their cheerful mind was singing
although sweat was on their brow.
Has all the humour left us! Why can't we whistle now?

Men in every walk of life whistled their way along
Their joyous laughter ringing and in their hearts a song
A man whistled in his garden working with his spade
We heard the mason whistling as he stones and mortar laid.
The Thatcher on the rooftop placing straws end to end
Whistled loud and cheerfully as he the scallops bent.
The servant sitting on his stool milking his patient cow
Whistled to her a merry tune. Why can't we whistle now?

Men whistled with their sleans and forks working in the bogs
They whistled drawing water and they whistled splitting logs
They whistled in the meadows as they tossed the fragrant hay
The mowers whetting the blades whistled the time away.
From County Council labourers spreading gravel on the roads
Came some merry whistling from their vibrant lips and throats
Men going to the creamery in their carts whistled too I vow
But we don't hear them anymore.
Why can't they whistle now?
The Drover whistled cheerfully driving cattle to the fair
The old man's lips were whistling
although confined to his chair
The cyclist whistled gaily as
he drove pedals up and down

The old age pensioner whistled
on his way to the post office in the town
The tailor whistled softly as he fitted on a suit
The cobbler whistled to himself stitching a patch onto a boot
The farmer whistled in the fields walking behind the plough
Oh God be with the good old days.
Why can't we whistle now?

We can't because we are imprisoned in tractor cabs and cars
Polluted from the stifling air of centrally heated bars
We're driving to the market, we're driving to the town
For turnips, spuds and cabbage we could have easily grown.
Lets get out into God's wholesome air
with our shovels, spade and hoe,
And put the furrows in our garden instead of on our brow
Then the gay spirit of the linnet and the lark in us will grow
And then like our forefathers maybe we can whistle now.

Clounleharde Stations 1977

During the time that Clounleharde National School was open the
Lenten Stations used to be held there annually for the people in the
southern end of the Parish of Ballyhahill. Then in 1967 the
Department of Education closed the school and the pupils were
taken to Ballyhahill. For a few years the stations were held in pri-
vate houses until this custom ended also. While all the stations held
in the houses were equally as homely and hospitable, the one at my
neighbours - O'Gradys house - has been recorded in verse.

'Twas the night after Patricks in 1977
We assembled at Jack Grady's to honour God up in Heaven
For here in Glenbawn in his homestead so grand
The Lenten Stations were held for the neighbouring townland.

Fr. Costelloe arrived with Jackie the Clerk
Whom our Holy Father with high honours had marked.
With everything in order the pleasant fire purred
Bringing comfort and warmth while confessions were heard.

While he donned his vestments to say Mass for the crowd
Father Costelloe recited the Rosary aloud.
During Mass he prayed for the living and dead
And asked God's blessings on the O'Grady homestead.

The sitting room, dining room, back kitchen and hall
Were filled with the neighbours who for Mass here did call.
In fact altogether they outnumbered two score
Yet there was a céad míle fáilte for each at the door.

When the Mass was then ended down at the table sat he
To collect any offerings for himself and the P.P.
For that night Fr. O'Regan had to leave us in the lurch
So as to receive Joe Mangan's remains in the Church.

The offerings being collected the tables were laid
With all kinds of goodies generously displayed
And there as an aftercourse what do you think
Bottles of stout for those who would drink.

But the best was to come when our bellies were filled
With lively entertainment the people were thrilled
Roger O Sullivan opened up with a song
Followed by Ned O' Shaughnessy and then came along

Our own loving curate in tremendous glee
Rendering "The Banks of my own Lovely Lee".
Then came Kit Brouder that Irish colleen
With a song in pure Gaelic, ár teanga blas binn.

This writer when asked gave a recitation he had
Of the love that united the Papist and Prod.
The angels in Heaven must surely feel proud
When saintly Peggie Egan stepped the hornpipe out.

From Jerry Wallace on the flute sweet music did come
Then Paddy Bawn followed on like a harmonium
Stephen Murphy from Glensharrold entertained us 'tis true
Head bowed with reverence, he sang "May Morning Dew".

From his fiancee Bridie Faley, after much coaxing came
The song of the picture in the golden frame.
For the grand finale the whole lot joined in
And hands joined together "Auld Lang Syne" we did sing.

They are "Jolly good fellows" so sang all of us
Meaning Jack and Peg and the children of course
And the whole night's proceedings ascended in prayer
To the angels in Heaven whom we hope to meet there.

St. John's Eve 1982
Tinekilla, Ballyhahill

'Twas the night of St. John's in 1982
The Comhaltas Ceólteóirí did our traditions renew
When at the cross of Tenekilla the bonfire did blaze
And the platform was set down our spirits to raise.

Reels, polkas and hornpipes were danced in great style
The old and the young there your heart would beguile
The roads all around with motors were lined
From all parts they came to revive the old times.

The minutes sped by and the crowd grew and grew
'Til the platform could no longer hold the whole crew
So enchanted were the people with the music's sweet note
They squared out and danced upon the tarred road.

Fond memories returned of a similar scene
Ere our eyes became glued to the TV screen
When at country crossroads when the days work was done
In crowds they'd assemble for some innocent fun.

Tonight our old custom is returning once more
And our cherished tradition we now have restored
What better entertainment can we bring along
Than our sweet Irish music and dancing and song?

Cheers for our Comhaltas – sure we can't go astray
With men like Michael Kearney to lead us on the way
Long may they live to enjoy the renown
And the fame they are bringing around their native town.

The Twin Lakes of Spahill (1990)

Some go to Lisdoonvarna for a dip in the spa water
To cure their arthritis and their pains and aches to slaughter
Since spa water effects a cure you'll find it nearer still
In superabundance it is found in the twin lakes of Spahill.

So don't you go travelling to far off Co. Clare
You'll find spa water in Knockdown, better than anywhere.
If you're suffering from lumbago or any other ill
You'll leave it all behind you in the twin lakes of Spahill.

No better place in Ireland to jump in for a swim
The magic of this water will loosen every limb
You'll go leaping o'er the heather with the joy it will instil
And you will count your blessings at the twin lakes of Spahill.

The peaceful surroundings will bring pleasure to your heart
Here your soul will find God's grace and you'll be loathe to part
There you can view a monument in the shape of a limekiln
That tells the tales of other days by the twin lakes of Spahill.

To this spot the sportsmen come with guns to try their luck
And have a shot at the pheasants, the woodcock and wild duck
You'll see the graceful seagulls floating on each rippling rill
That dances on the surface of the twin lakes of Spahill.

So if ever you are travelling along the Kerryline
In one of our hot summers when the sun decides to shine
Take the bog road by Ned Shaughnessy's
your dreams you will fulfil
And go home bouncing like a hare from the twin lakes of Spahill.

The tourists will soon be flocking when the good news gets around
That miraculous cures in Spahill water has recently been found
Then Government grants we will be seeking -
get them I know we will
To improve the amenities around the twin lakes of Spahill.

A Tribute to Ballyhahill (1985)

Back through the years of G.A.A. since 1884
Great men shone out upon the field that thrilled spectators o'er
In that roll of fame and honour our locals had a share
For in many a triumphant battle, Ballyhahill lads were there.

From out this worthy parish went men of brains and brawn
Who were a credit to their people around silvery Abha Bhán
To promote our Irish culture in countries everywhere
And hoist the flag of victory, Ballyhahill lads were there.

'Tis with pride we can look back across the waves of time
When our emigrants undaunted fought their way in many a clime
And proved their worth and Irish blood and talents rich and rare
To the fore among them, Ballyhahill lads were there.

Preserving our rich culture here in our native isle
Our traditional music, dance and song in typical Irish style
Is nurtured and growing healthily in this place beyond compare
For in everything that's Irish, Ballyhahill lads were there.

In Comhaltas Ceolteorí Éireann they are a shining light
What wonderful entertainment to the community they provide
Watching them on R.T.É there was no better anywhere
When it came to dance the polka set, the Ballyhahill lads were there.

In many competitions how well they have engaged
Revealing their Gaelic talents outstanding shows they've staged
And won tumultuous applause as hearts they did ensnare
To receive All-Ireland honours, Ballyhahill lads were there.

When the voice of God was calling for vocations for his church
It didn't fall on deaf ears here, He was not left in the lurch
Among the ordained priests of God given to his care
To teach and preach His gospel, Ballyhahill lads were there.

Our ladies too have played their part with football and camán
And into deserving organisations their noble work is drawn
In helping the less fortunate themselves they do not spare
Wherever they can do noble work, Ballyhahill girls are there.

When Mother Ireland was molested by the foreigners' cruel hand
To save her from her enemy our patriots took their stand
Among that true and trusted band whose allegiance did swear
To strike a blow for freedom, Ballyhahill lads were there.

To foster our Irish games was wanted a patch of land
They could develop into a sporting pitch with dressing rooms and
stand
To finance the project was no joke but the committee did not despair
Rising to the occasion, the Ballyhahill lads were there.

With this field now our ambitious youth can find themselves secure
We hope the spirits of their fathers for centuries will endure
To keep the colours flying and their minds free of dull care
To ensure future generations, Ballyhahill will be there.

When the final whistle blows and our last game is played
And up before St. Peter in true colours we're arrayed
To receive our worthwhile trophy a place in Heaven to share
In that great roll of honour, Ballyhahill will be there.

Mass at Ath na gCorp, Clounleharde

On the 17th day of August in the year 2001
To an unmarked grave in Clounleharde
many people there did throng
Where a Mass was concelebrated, God to praise and honour
By P.P. Fr. O Leary and local man Fr. Michael O Connor.

In 1580, in this sacred spot was buried in the clay
Some of the 400 massacred who had fled for safety there.
Pelham and his forces, led there by McShane,
Found them huddled in the wood, all devoutly praying.

The only life that was saved was a girl named O'Dowd
Whom McShane was eager to marry but she would not allow it
Some hours after the massacre he forced her with him back again
While he searched for valuables through the pockets of the slain.

As he was bent down thus engaged he laid his battleaxe aside
She picked it up and with one blow his skull she opened wide.
History has recorded that later on in life
A man named Dore from Glin took her as his bride.

So to remember this occasion many people gathered round
Patie Flavin had prepared the place with a wooden bridge laid down
The altar Fr. Tim set up was bedecked with fresh cut flowers
And Caitriona's music on the concert flute kept quiet the threatened
showers

This place will ever hold the memory of our sorrowful history
When our forefathers were subjected
to such cruel deaths and misery.

With courage they bore it with
their faith in God and his Blessed Son
And upheld their Christian values
in spite of oppressors sword and gun
Let us pray that here today our faith forever more will thrive
That faith our forefathers fought for and died to keep alive.

Peace and Goodwill

As I looked out my window at bedtime last night
And gazed at the heavenly sphere
I saw how unselfish the moon shone her light
To brighten this world down here.

And there all around her were millions of stars
And I thought on the Creator's skill
And I dreamed of men fighting devastating wars
Forgetting all peace and goodwill.

My thoughts dwelt on the quiet and peace up above
With everything in rhythm and tune
And the stars looked like children reflecting the love
As it beamed from their mother the moon.

And if only God's children would look up and pray
His own Love in their hearts to instil
Like the moon and the stars we'd have here today
Freedom and peace and goodwill.

My Gift of Rhyming

I didn't get the gift of music, neither can I sing
My feet weren't made for dancing
that so much pleasure to others bring.
Still my mind is cheerful and my days are always bright
For the gift I got of rhyming with words is my delight.

In God's world that nature cares there's music song and dance
In the flora and the fauna I see love and romance.
Then words come freely to me
to express my thoughts in rhyme
God's earthly things all seem to speak and sanctify my time.

In some songs that I have written how delightful then to hear
Their words being set to music to bring pleasure to the ear
Of others not so fortunate who got no gifts to use the pen
For putting words together to cheer their fellowman.

So to God I'm really thankful for the gift I did obtain
I hope I'll always use it His goodness to proclaim
For to Him is due the credit for everything I own
May He guide my every footstep
as through this life I'm going.

The Life and Rhymes of Paddy Faley

The Life and Rhymes of Paddy Faley